Florian A. Gebler

When Darkness Falls
the Stars Appear

Florian A. Gebler

When Darkness Falls the Stars Appear

Reflections on Life and Mortality

Bibliographic Information of the German National Library:
The German National Library lists this publication in the German National Bibliography; detailed bibliographic data can be accessed online at http://dnb.dnb.de

The original edition was published under the title:
Wenn der Tod anklopft sieht man die Sterne in der Nacht. Reflexionen über Leben und Sterben.
Copyright © 2024 by Quellwasser Verlag, Schwangau, Germany

English Edition, 1st Edition:
© 2024 by Quellwasser Verlag, Schwangau, Germany

Typesetting and Design: Florian A. Gebler
Cover Image: shutterstock, ID: 1237579327, C. Luangrangwech
Printed: Libri Plureos GmbH, Friedensallee 273, 22763 Hamburg

ISBN: 978-3-939641-05-6

Inhalt

Introduction

At the age of 45, death knocked at my door. A few days after a routine check-up, I received a call from my general practitioner, and she immediately confronted me with the news: "You have a plasmacytoma!" I had no idea what it meant, but the tone of her words was deeply unsettling. Her brief explanation sounded suspiciously like cancer, though she never uttered the word. After the call, I was left feeling agitated and uncertain—the true meaning of the diagnosis still eluded me. I hesitated to consult Google, fully aware that the internet is rarely a reliable guide for health matters. Yet despite my reservations, my thirst for answers won out. I skimmed through several entries and quickly discovered that plasmacytoma and multiple myeloma were often synonymous. When I came across an entry stating that the average life expectancy for multiple myeloma was 3-5 years after diagnosis, I stopped my research. I was in shock.

Still, the diagnosis wasn't entirely unexpected. For months, even years, I had endured significant physical symptoms. I had suffered from persistent joint pain, so severe that I was tested for gout and rheumatoid arthritis, both of which yielded negative results. I was frequently fatigued, drained of energy and motivation, and for a long time, even picking up a book in the evening required tremendous effort. Surprisingly, I had learned to live with my symptoms. I rationalized them as normal, attributing them to lack of sleep due to my children, my advancing age, or a Lyme disease diagnosis (which I received due to my joint pain and a positive test result, in the absence of other explanations). With the diagnosis, many of these symptoms suddenly took on a new and ominous meaning. In hindsight, perhaps I should have paid closer attention to them earlier.

Yet there was something else—a dark premonition from my childhood, now seemingly coming to life. As a child in elementary school, I attended a three-week summer camp in South Tyrol alone. One evening, with three other kids, I participated in a playful "ghost summoning." We summoned an anonymous spirit to answer our questions. I still don't know what prompted me, but with a mix of boldness and childish naiveté, I asked when and how I would die. The answer was: At 44, from cancer. On the surface, I dismissed it as nonsense, comforted by the fact that 44 seemed so far away in my young mind. Yet deep down, the memory left a mark, often buried but resurfacing from time to time. I grew up to become a rational adult, and eventually, a scientifically-minded psychologist. Whenever the memory resurfaced, I rationalized it away and pushed it aside. I felt a sense of relief when I reached my 45th birthday, believing I had finally laid the memory to rest. Yet six months later, I received the cancer diagnosis, and the memory, with all its uncertainty, came rushing back. Was it a coincidence? I had survived 44, but the proximity was unsettling—could there be truth in that prediction after all? Or was it a self-fulfilling prophecy? Had the cancer developed in the fertile ground of my subconscious fears? I found no answers, but I put the questions aside, as more urgent matters took priority.

Multiple myeloma is a form of cancer that affects plasma cells in the bone marrow. Plasma cells, a type of white blood cell, play a crucial role in the immune system by producing specific antibodies that combat infections. In multiple myeloma, abnormal plasma cells multiply uncontrollably, producing excessive monoclonal antibodies, which are useless for their normal immune function. The disease manifests in various ways, with symptoms such as fatigue, lack of drive, anemia, a weakened immune system, increased susceptibility to infections, bone pain leading to bone erosion and fractures, impaired kidney function, and elevated calcium levels in the blood. Although the prognosis has improved significantly in recent years, multiple myeloma is still considered a chronic, incurable disease. Treatment aims to slow the progression of the disease and prolong life. Current cancer research holds the promise that one day, the disease may be curable, though similar hopes have been raised before, only to remain unrealized. Cancer continues to carry an aura of dread and darkness.

This book chronicles my search for healing, my intense confrontation with the looming presence of death, and my quest for the meaning of life. My aim was to find a perspective that not only acknowledges the terror of illness but also reveals its potential value. Illness brings destruction, yet it also offers the opportunity for positive change and inner growth. The diagnosis, along with the threat of death, forced me to reassess my life and make changes. The reflections and changes it prompted have proven invaluable to me. I hope my experiences and reflections will offer encouragement and inspire others to confront illness and death while there is still time for life and transformation. This confrontation need not be negative or desperate—hope persists, even when physical recovery remains uncertain. As Vaclav Havel said, "Hope is not the conviction that something will turn out well, but the certainty that something is meaningful, regardless of how it turns out."

I write this book not as an expert, but as someone personally affected. These are my personal experiences and thoughts—it is not a prescription for dealing with illness and death. I believe every person must find their own path, and that there is no right or wrong way. Each person, each life situation, each illness is different. At the same time, this book is more than just a personal account. My longstanding engagement with philosophical and spiritual themes forms the backdrop of my reflections. In this book, I often draw upon philosophical and spiritual ideas that have surfaced during my current situation. These thoughts have been both inspiring and fruitful for me, and I wish to share them with others.

This book, along with the reflections it offers on life and death, remains unfinished. I started writing this book shortly after my diagnosis, when my experiences and reflections were still fresh and unfiltered. It serves as a snapshot of my current experiences, thoughts, and inspirations. As I wrote, new thoughts, experiences, and impulses continued to emerge, which I sought to include, even if they didn't always fit into the existing text. A book requires an ending, even though my journey continues. Lastly, this book remains unfinished because I have yet to overcome my illness and the looming threat of death. I also don't believe that illness and death can ever be fully "overcome"—that one can reach a point of final resolution, free from anxiety and despair. They reappear in different forms and present new challenges each time. They are part of our life journey, and I see it as a lifelong task to face them with courage. I draw hope from the existential experiences of others and hope that this book can, in turn, be a source of courage and hope for others.

Into the Crucible

Multiple myeloma is a serious illness, yet my experience as a patient was somewhat privileged: at that time, I endured little pain or physical limitations. Even so, I was profoundly shaken. Confronting death is no small thing. The threat of death brought with it anxiety and a sense of loss. With the cancer diagnosis, the certainty of an open future vanished instantly—along with the future I had envisioned with my loved ones. My dreams and life goals suddenly seemed fragile and distant, possibly slipping beyond my reach. The path before me was no longer guided by my desires and aspirations, but now seemed dictated by the illness and the inevitable treatments. Beyond that lay a diffuse, impenetrable fog; whether my path continued beyond it was uncertain.

I felt a widening chasm between myself and the healthy people around me, who went about their routines, concerns, and plans as though the future were assured. It felt as though an invisible divide had formed between the living and myself—a condemned man, whose days were numbered. The thoughts that crossed my mind didn't seem suited for light conversation, nor did I feel a desire for superficial encounters. I longed to speak authentically, yet I didn't know how. I felt constrained. I feared the fragility of my thoughts and my inner world. The reflections that came to me in grappling with my mortality became precious to me. Revealing these thoughts would mean exposing them to others, risking dismissal, and thereby devaluing them. I felt the need to guard my thoughts, making me cautious and selective about who I trusted with deeper conversations. I had the impression that I was living in a different world than those around me, and it was hard to bridge those worlds.

Though I felt a sense of inner strength and made decisions autonomously, my vulnerability remained ever-present. My decision to pursue a complementary medicine approach made me vulnerable, as it was not well-received by conventional medicine. My choice was met with at least doubt, if not outright dismissal, by official authorities and many of my peers. While I felt strong and confident in my decision, I was aware of its uncertainty. There was no recognized authority I could rely on to justify my choice. I had the feeling that others saw me as foolish and naïve, constantly forcing me to justify my decision. As a result, I avoided discussing my illness and withdrew somewhat from social activities.

Becoming aware of my body's fragility was also a painful experience. I had always had an athletic, capable body, and even at 45, I could still cling to the illusion of youth. Now, I was acutely aware of its vulnerability and lost faith in its reliability. I could no longer trust that my body would sustain me as it always had. My greatest fear, however, wasn't death itself, but the thought of becoming frail and dependent. I feared the prospect of lingering in pain, bedridden and dependent on others. I feared not being able to care for my loved ones anymore, instead becoming a burden to them.

A fracture seemed to run through my sense of time, my relationships, and my connection to my body. It pained me to imagine missing out on the future paths of my family and friends—that they might continue their lives without me. It pained me to think of plans and ideas I had saved for later, which might never come to fruition. It pained me to be inwardly separated from people who were physically close to me but living in a different world. I confronted both the anxiety of death and the anxiety of guilt—the guilt of an unlived life. I also grappled with the anxiety of freedom. For example, the anxiety that arises from freely and independently choosing a treatment path—despite all the uncertainty and doubt—with the realization that I might lose my life if I make the wrong choice.

What I hadn't anticipated was the challenge of remaining aware of my life-threatening situation. The illness felt surreal, and it would have been all too easy to push aside thoughts of illness and death. This was a critical point. On a fundamental level, ignoring my reality and doing nothing posed a true threat to my life. I had to confront my illness and, at the very least, decide on the best possible treatment option. Beyond that, I also wanted to engage with the deeper meaning of my illness because I sensed there was more to it. It felt like my "trial by fire." In my work as an existentially oriented psychologist, I had spent years grappling with suffering, death, and anxiety. I had spoken with many patients about the importance of facing one's own mortality. But now, I found myself standing face-to-face with it. Would my years of theoretical engagement truly provide a foundation for navigating this real experience?

One of the first questions that pressed on me was: Why shouldn't I die? By modern standards, I was not old, and my children still needed me. But by other standards, I had already reached a blessed age. I was aware that countless people had to die much younger, without the fortune of living 45 broadly untroubled years. People whose lives were cut short by illness, accidents, or wars they didn't choose. Shouldn't I feel grateful for having lived this life?

A few weeks ago, a friend told me about his parents, who were over 90, nearly blind, and increasingly immobile—and for years, they had not wanted to live anymore. In light of this, the often-desired goal of living as long as possible didn't seem particularly appealing. People must die; that is the natural order of things, and that's a good thing. But for oneself, it is hard to submit to this natural order. Of course, I wanted to keep living—I didn't feel my life had run its course just yet. But I also didn't want to desperately cling to a life I might later wish to let go of. A saying came to mind: "The aim isn't to add years to life, but life to years." While this saying has become somewhat cliché, it still resonated deeply with me. If my life was worth saving from this illness—if I were to be granted more years—it had to be a life filled with vitality. But was it?

Until now, my life had been blessed, and there was so much for which I felt profoundly grateful. I had a wonderful wife and three amazing, healthy children. For the most part, we enjoyed a harmonious and carefree family life. I had the freedom to shape my career path, to study, and I always found fulfilling work. In every professional position, I received recognition and appreciation. We had a beautiful, spacious home, and we didn't face any real financial worries, even though career and money were never our top priorities. I had good friends and many talents. For all of this—and so much more—I had always felt a deep sense of gratitude. I had always known that none of it was guaranteed, and I was content with my life, as I told anyone who asked. But was it truly a life filled with vitality?

I've spent a lot of time reflecting on when I've felt truly alive in my life. I've asked myself what the markers of a vibrant and fulfilling life might be. Words like joy, energy, passion, drive, and a profound conviction that what you're doing is exactly right came to mind. I realized that in recent years, I hadn't felt these things much. I often felt unmotivated, lacking real energy, lethargic, and devoid of enthusiasm. I had to force myself to get through many tasks and activities. To feel truly alive must be something quite different. I reflected on my life's path, questioning whether I had been on the right one in recent years. Pindar's call to "Become who you are" weighed heavily on me. Had I followed my heart in recent years? Or had I been too afraid, falling into a materialistic mindset that, for me, was tightly bound to the responsibilities of fatherhood. In recent years, financial security had taken on growing importance to me, something I hadn't previously given much thought. But with children, material stability became more central: healthy food, a spacious and healthy home, good clothing, education, sports, insurance, outings, vacations, and so on—money seemed to slip through our fingers. And even though my wife, Julia, and I were both working and earning a decent income, it often didn't feel like enough. Increasingly, small financial concerns weighed on me, and financial stability took on greater importance.

I felt as though my life had somehow shifted into "waiting mode." My interests and dreams were largely "on hold," postponed for times when I wasn't working or meeting family obligations. Then there was the ongoing lack of energy that had worn me down in the evenings. By the time the children were finally in bed, I was ready for bed myself. I hoped for more time and energy for my interests and dreams once the children grew older.

A Bible verse came to mind, where a rich man, having finally filled his barns, thought he could now rest and enjoy his life, to which God said, "Thou fool, this night thy soul shall be required of thee: then whose shall those things be, which thou hast provided?" (Luke 12:20). I felt like I had somehow strayed onto the same path. I had relied too much on an open future, postponing important things, and, in doing so, had strayed from my true path. I wasn't currently on the path to becoming who only I could become. The cancer diagnosis jolted me awake: I could no longer live my life in waiting mode, as my future was now uncertain.

Shortly afterward, I received yet another reminder of this theme's significance. I had a molar extracted—a tooth whose root had become infected and died over 20 years ago, which had been treated with a root canal to save it. The tooth hadn't given me any real problems over the years and continued to function, but I had read years ago that root canal-treated teeth can secretly cause significant health issues. Given the severity of my illness, I didn't want to take any risks and decided to remove this potential source of harm. During the extraction, it was revealed that two large cysts had formed beneath the roots. In a book on *Teeth and Spagyric Medicine*, I later read that my affected tooth symbolized the need to rediscover one's life plan and to ask how one's life was truly meant to be. It was said to be a subconscious distress signal, warning that I was on the brink of missing my life's purpose and true path. I had to admit that this hit very close to home. The question of my purpose and destiny weighed on me, but despite much reflection, I initially found only fragmentary answers.

I yearned for healing. But what did healing truly mean? As strange as the question may sound, the answer is complex and challenging. Of course, I wanted to recover physically, to overcome the illness, and to spend many more years free of pain and in good health. But that was only the superficial dimension. If healing is seen as a form of positive development, then the illness itself held healing within it, as it was a blend of both negative and positive aspects. My illness was, in a sense, paradoxical. Based on test results, I was suddenly diagnosed with a serious illness. Up until those results, I had been officially healthy, and I would have considered myself healthy, despite having suffered from various ailments for some time. On average, I hadn't felt great before the diagnosis, but I had considered myself healthy and was officially classified as such. After the diagnosis, I made some changes in my life, particularly in my diet and habits. As a result, my health improved significantly. Within a week, for example, I no longer had joint pain, and my mental clarity also improved greatly. I felt really good, but now I was officially sick. I was often unsure how to describe myself. Remarkably, I had come to terms with my symptoms before. They had bothered me and affected me, but I had, for the most part, rationalized them as "normal." Of course, I knew that diet could have a major impact on my health, but since I had been paying close attention to my diet for some time, I didn't expect that a more radical change would make a significant difference. But what surprised me in hindsight was that I had never tried. Looking back, it would have been relatively simple, but I had been too lethargic—it hadn't seemed worth the effort, even though the health problems were limiting. It was only the cancer diagnosis that gave me the impetus to take that step. With these changes, I felt physically better than I had before the diagnosis. In that sense, I found myself grateful for the diagnosis. Yet the potential for positive transformation went much deeper.

Not only had I rationalized my physical discomfort, but, as previously mentioned, the illness painfully exposed a deeper emptiness in my life, even if I couldn't fully pinpoint what it was. My life lacked enthusiasm, joy, drive, and purpose. But I had accepted that as normal too, under the conviction that it couldn't be changed in the current circumstances. I felt somewhat trapped by the duties of a father trying to always be there for his family. But was that truly normal and unchangeable? The diagnosis and the looming threat of death jolted me, challenging my previous beliefs. I might not have much time left. If I were to die soon, my family would have to find their way without me—and they surely would. So, couldn't I claim a bit more freedom while I was still alive, even if it meant I wouldn't always be there for my family? It had been hard for me to carve out time for myself in recent years, especially since Julia had just as little, if not less, time for herself. Our youngest son wasn't independent enough yet; one of us had to be present, which bound us not only physically but also mentally.

A terminal illness brings with it a sense of: now or never. It legitimizes focusing more on myself and paying attention to my own needs. But this, too, was an ambivalent matter. I refused to identify as sick. When people asked me how I was doing, I refused to say I was sick. Even though it may have seemed like a mere linguistic nuance to others, I didn't want to identify my "being" with sickness by saying, "I am sick." I would usually answer, "I'm doing well," or if I had to address it, I would say, "I've been diagnosed with cancer." After all, what I had received, I could also get rid of. I didn't want to label myself as sick, and, in fact, I felt healthier than I had in a long time. But on the other hand, the diagnosis was real, and I had to do something to get well again. For that, I needed the diagnosis and the accompanying label of "sick," as it gave me the social legitimacy to take the time I needed for myself and my treatment.

For me, illness as a crisis contained both danger and the possibility for positive change. In my work as a psychologist, I often defended illness against the prejudice that it was purely negative and something to be battled. I was a follower of Viktor E. Frankl, who described humans as "Homo patients,"—the suffering human. Suffering is part of human life, sooner or later; we cannot keep it out of our lives. The question is not whether we will suffer, but how. What matters is how we deal with suffering and illness and what we make of it. Severe illness often serves as a catalyst, prompting us to question our lives, reexamine what is truly important, and find new direction.

In my conversations with patients, I sometimes shared a saying, which I believe originates from the Persian poet and mystic Rumi: The soul and the body meet, and the soul laments that its owner doesn't listen to it. The body responds: "I have an idea. I will become sick, and then he will have time for you." I always found this saying helpful in dealing with illness. Viewed this way, illness becomes a call for introspection, a prompt to connect with oneself and one's own fragile inner voice. Illness gives us time for ourselves and for reconnecting with our soul. It's not always about overcoming illness as quickly as possible, just to continue living as we did before. Illness also calls for reflection, reorientation, and change.

From this perspective, illness is not a weakness but simply another way of being, with its own unique possibilities and limitations. A way of being that can also hold value and meaning. I often feel that this isn't acknowledged in our achievement-oriented society, where illness is seen solely as negative and meaningless. Only strength and productivity are considered worthy. Many people uncritically embrace and perpetuate Schopenhauer's famous quote: "Health is not everything, but without health, everything is nothing." Without health, this implies illness, and thus, with illness, everything becomes meaningless. If cancer is a severe chronic illness, then I must be facing nothingness; my life becomes worthless and meaningless.

People often quote the Roman poet Juvenal's phrase: "Mens sana in corpore sano" ("A sound mind in a sound body"). This aligns with a philosophy focused on physical capability, and it's no coincidence that this phrase was prominent in National Socialist ideology. A sound mind and a sound body go hand in hand, it seems. But what if one is missing? If I am physically ill, can I have a sound mind? Or is it my mind that's preventing my body from being healthy? This line of thinking can lead to dangerous places. Ultimately, it's clear where the focus lies in this quote—on health and strength. However, the perspective shifts when you know that the common translation is misleading, as it's taken out of context. What Juvenal actually meant was the opposite. He was critical of body worship and said, "Pray that there is also a sound mind in a sound body." A healthy body is important, but so is a healthy mind—and the two don't always go hand in hand. There are those of remarkable physical strength who are, in many ways, morally and psychologically deficient, displaying traits like selfishness and malice. Conversely, there are those with chronic illness or disability whose character and mental resilience make them shining examples, earning my profound admiration.

In our culture, productivity and achievement often overshadow our approach to life and purpose. These values are complemented by prestige, a sense of order, and cleanliness. All of these are valuable, but are they enough for a fulfilling life? I'm reminded of a story where a meditation master, traveling through France with a student, sees a cemetery through the train window. The student exclaims in awe, "Look at that! Even the cemeteries here are more beautiful and well-kept than the houses back home!" The master replies, "That's true. I just wish they took care of their souls as well as they do their cemeteries."

Those who know the children's book Frederick understand that the diligent, practical mindset of gathering and achieving contrasts with a contemplative, artistic approach to living that is equally valuable. I'm not arguing for an "either-or" here, where one way of life is better than the other. Both are important and complement each other. However, severe physical illness makes it difficult, if not impossible, to be active and productive. Those who are ill often lose access to society's values of productivity. What remains is the invaluable inward path—a journey of contemplation and reflection. These have intrinsic value, yet they are often neglected or sorely lacking in our society. In this sense, illness can provide a healing counterbalance to the relentless busyness of society. It's about caring for the soul.

For many years, I worked as a clinical psychologist in psychosomatic rehabilitation. Many of my patients were unable to work due to their conditions, often for extended periods. They were no longer productive or capable, and they didn't fit into society or the current workforce. Yet, I was constantly moved by how remarkable my patients were. Many were intelligent, sensitive, courageous, and morally upright individuals. In my work, I was often reminded of an Indian guru's statement: Health cannot be measured by how well one adjusts to a profoundly sick society. Yet, this is precisely how mental health is defined: In our society, the "healthy" person is the one who conforms to the norm (defined by statistical averages). On the flip side, I occasionally heard my patients ask, "So, who is truly unwell—us, or the society around us?" You can find the same thought in Friedrich Nietzsche's philosophy: "The person who lies sick in bed sometimes realizes that it is, in fact, his usual office, business, or social life that makes him unwell, causing him to lose all clarity about himself; he gains this insight from the stillness his illness imposes upon him."

On a deeper level, the line between health and illness becomes blurred. Defining someone as sick or healthy involves culturally determined criteria that don't necessarily have to be accepted as they are. What is healing? Should my aim really be to help my wonderful, sensitive patients adapt to a harsh, unhealthy work environment—even if it means they must become hardened and more self-centered?

Given these reflections, the question arises: can we truly recognize and appreciate the value of illness? Serious illness is often linked to a loss of productivity, yet it teaches us the value of leisure. The threat of death is not life's enemy; rather, awareness of mortality strengthens our sense of life's value. Etty Hillesum writes in her diary: "If you deny death, life is never complete, and by including death in your life, you expand and enrich it." Irvin Yalom, reflecting on his work with terminally ill cancer patients, shares a similar insight, rephrasing a realization from his patients: It's a pity that I had to wait until my body was ravaged by cancer to learn how to live. Yalom describes how these individuals suddenly found the courage to reassess their priorities, focusing solely on what they truly desired and living more intensely, with greater appreciation for life's everyday moments.

All these reflections made it clear to me that healing extends far beyond physical recovery. Of course, I, too, wish for health and regard it as an extremely valuable asset worth protecting and preserving. I seek healing because I want to live—not merely exist, but to live actively. I still have plans and dreams, many of which are only achievable if I am physically capable. Nonetheless, I fully agree with Schipperges when he writes: "Health is by no means the highest good, but rather a vital medium for one's own creative, meaningful existence." Health is important, but it should serve values that go beyond it. At times, health is essential for realizing these values; at others, it is not. Sometimes, these values reveal themselves through illness—in how I respond to my illness. I didn't want to cling desperately to physical recovery; instead, I wanted to open myself to healing in all its dimensions.

In my early adulthood, I read Stephen Levine's *Healing into Life and Death*. It was about the spiritual support of terminally ill cancer patients, with a focus on spiritual healing. Levine wrote about end-stage patients who experienced spiritual healing and, as a result, also recovered physically. But he also saw many patients who experienced spiritual healing and still passed away. The book left a profound impact on me, deeply moving and shaping my perspective. At its core was the idea that healing can take place, even in death.

If many people experience physical healing after spiritual healing, that alone would be enough reason to pursue spiritual healing. However, if this were my only motivation for spiritual healing, I would reduce it to a mere tool, stripping it of its meaning and power. It would become merely a means to an end, with physical healing taking precedence. The danger, then, would be that I might feel disappointed and view my healing as a failure if physical recovery didn't follow. That wasn't my path. For me, soul healing became the true focal point. With these reflections in mind, I was acutely aware of my fundamental mortality. Even if I overcame this illness, there would inevitably come a day when I would lose my health and face death. Even in recovery, I could face a serious accident tomorrow, leading to severe impairment or death—a possibility my work in a large trauma hospital constantly reminded me of. Thus, prioritizing my spiritual integrity and a holistic approach to healing seemed both more reliable and meaningful.

The term "spiritual healing" may sound abstract or even lofty. So, what is spiritual healing? Again, the answer is not simple. For me, there is a worldly side and a religious-spiritual side. In scientific psychology, terms like "soul" have been replaced by "behavior, experience, and consciousness," making the soul more objectively measurable and accessible. That's the worldly side. But how should healing be defined here? The goal of efforts cannot be the "norm," as defined by societal averages. I believe it can only represent an "Idea" of what it means to be human—a vision of what a person should strive to become. For my own healing, it's not about an abstract, general idea of humanity—it's about my personal vision of myself, of who I should be and want to become. Both my worldly and spiritual paths to healing will serve as the focus of the reflections that follow.

Becoming Who I Am

A key part of my healing was realizing my true essence—becoming the person only I could become. This idea is vividly expressed in the words of the Hasidic Rabbi Susya: "When I get to heaven, they will not ask me: Why weren't you Moses? Instead, they will ask: Why weren't you Susya? Why didn't you become the person only you could be?" But who was I? Who am I at the core of my being, and who do I want to become? Despite my psychotherapeutic training and the self-reflection it entailed, I found it difficult to answer these questions.

My cancer diagnosis shook the familiar answers that come to mind for such questions. If the disease were to take a severe course, I would likely face significant pain and limitations. In my mind, I imagined myself bedridden, unable to fulfill my roles as partner, father, friend, and therapist—roles and activities that give me purpose and identity. Who am I, then, when I am no longer able to do anything, when I no longer serve any function? This perspective called my current self-image into question entirely. In that future, little would remain except me—my essence—and the hope for meaningful connections reaching from that core to the world around me, to the people I love, and to God, the foundation of all being.

For now, I was still fit; I felt physically and mentally capable. I still had the potential to change and shape the world around me. So, who was I at the core of my being, and how could I realize it? At its core, it was about self-knowledge. But how does one achieve self-knowledge? One condition is that I need to be in a good relationship with myself. It sounds simple and self-evident. Of course, we're always in a relationship with ourselves, just as we are when we're with others. But it is also part of our experience that we can feel utterly alone and disconnected, even in the middle of a crowd. In the same way, our relationship with ourselves can feel empty and meaningless. Relationships become real and fulfilling only when we are truly present in them—when we take time for the other and approach them with mindfulness. When we genuinely try to understand the other. In the busy flow of daily life, filled with tasks and distractions, it's challenging to experience truly meaningful relationships. For instance, I often struggled to give my children the attention they deserved. I was often too absorbed in my own thoughts and the distractions of daily life. I was often dissatisfied with myself and the way I related to my children. Likewise, being in a good relationship with myself was just as challenging.

Uninterrupted moments of connection with myself had been rare long before the diagnosis, and when they did occur, I often struggled to make meaningful use of them. Like so many others, my daily life before the diagnosis was shaped by work at the clinic and the usual family routine. I usually left the house at 6:30 in the morning and returned at 6:00 in the evening. Then there was dinner and some household chores, followed by putting the children to bed. The time afterward was often "empty"; I spent it on my smartphone or occasionally watching a movie. Occasionally, I would read a bit, but never quite enough. Julia was often in the same state, lying next to me on the sofa with her tablet. We spent time together, yet we weren't truly connected. The windows for quality time were fewer than we would have liked, and we lacked the energy to change that or make better use of our time together. Our time was always filled, but not always fulfilling.

Without regular, intimate connection with ourselves, we cannot truly know who we are, and we begin to wither inwardly. Getting to know someone truly takes time and attention—two of the most valuable gifts we can offer anyone. So, am I worth offering myself that time and attention? Or is it the opposite—that we'd rather avoid such encounters? In his book *Eden Culture*, Johannes Hartl (8) describes an experiment that shows how uncomfortable it seems for us to simply spend time with ourselves. In this experiment, students were asked to do nothing for 15 minutes, simply to be alone with their thoughts. However, if they wished, they could give themselves mild, yet painful electric shocks as a distraction. Surprisingly, most chose the shocks. Apparently, we'd rather subject ourselves to painful distractions than spend time alone with ourselves. It wasn't that bad for me. Generally, I enjoyed being alone, but often it didn't seem important enough, as I usually filled my free time with other activities.

My diagnosis helped me distance myself from these "disruptions of relationship" as the threat of death shifted my awareness. A particular thought exercise proved helpful: I tried to regularly remind myself that this moment could be my last—my last spring, my last workday, my last time doing "this or that"—and if so, how would I want to experience it? What would really matter? The answer was usually simple: as mindfully as possible, free from distraction, fully present in the here and now, appreciating whatever was with me in that moment. In those "last time" moments, the wind on my skin felt precious, as did the scent of spring and the soft rays of sunlight filtering through the trees. Or my children's laughter, their stories about their day, or simply playing with them. These were the truly valuable things in my life. Albert Camus' *The Stranger* presents a similar experience. The protagonist, condemned to death, waits in his cell for the sentence to be carried out. As he glimpses a square of blue sky through the skylight, he feels that, for the first time in his life, he truly sees it. Of course, he had seen the sky countless times before, but now he was truly able to perceive it. The threat of death can make us perceive life with mindfulness. Mindfulness shapes how we experience reality. It connects us deeply with life, sharpening our awareness of the everyday things we often take for granted.

This heightened mindfulness alone brought a profound change to my life; everything felt much more alive. In principle, mindfulness wasn't new to me. As a psychotherapist, I often incorporated mindfulness exercises in my work. Yet in my daily life, I found it difficult to maintain a continuous state of mindfulness. Mindfulness isn't something you can possess, like an object. It remains fragile, delicate, and vulnerable. Life is usually filled with distractions and judgments, with motives anchored in the past or the future. Yet when I consciously reminded myself of my finite time through the thought exercise above, returning to a mindful state felt easier. When I was in such intense contact with myself and the world, each moment felt alive and valuable. I could more fully appreciate the value of ordinary daily experiences. It was no longer, "Vacuuming again—how annoying!" but, "Thank God I can still vacuum without pain! I am part of life, and this moment is precious!"

Even in my professional life, this mindful attitude, shaped by my awareness of mortality, led to change. For some time before the diagnosis, I hadn't felt fully satisfied with my work. While I experienced many rewarding moments as a psychotherapist and received positive feedback, I often doubted whether my work was genuinely meaningful. I often felt that some of my core abilities weren't fully utilized in this role, even though using them would have brought me joy. For instance, I believe I have a particular talent for identifying the essence of issues in discussions, distilling them to their core, and finding appropriate solutions. I can think systematically and analytically and work well with numbers. For a time, I was able to use these skills as Head Psychologist at a psychosomatic rehabilitation clinic, but I grew increasingly frustrated with a system that allowed only superficial, short-sighted solutions and little room for deep engagement with problems. There was simply no time for more; everything was dictated by the constraints of short-term profitability, regardless of its impact on employees or patients. So, I decided to throw in the towel and took a new job without a leadership role. Some aspects have improved, but the fundamental issues remain. I struggle with our healthcare system, which functions more as a "sickness system," with more profit to be made from illness than from health. In this system, the commercial director holds more influence than the medical director, with profit placed above all else. I had often thought about how I might escape this system and find a field where my other skills could be put to better use. But I hadn't found any solutions, and I have to admit, I often gave up too quickly. Given my family's financial security, any change would only be feasible with the right financial conditions. Overall, my current professional situation was that I wasn't unhappy, but I wasn't fully satisfied either. Nor had I yet found a vision for change.

Mindfulness somewhat altered my perception of my current professional role too. I became newly aware of how privileged I was to be able to do this work. I was reminded of how fortunate I was to have learned a profession that suited my nature, rather than one that went against it. A job I didn't just have to do to survive, but one where I could find fulfillment. In my current work, I had the privilege of encountering people daily, with many of these encounters being genuine and authentic. For a brief time, people revealed themselves to me in all their vulnerability—with their troubles, fears, losses, mistakes, and the delicate nuances of human life, showing both its depths as well as its courage and dignity. My job allowed me to peek beneath society's surface, beyond the polished appearances typically presented to the outside world. I was given the chance to witness real life. At times, I feel as though I've become almost addicted to these kinds of encounters, finding little satisfaction in more superficial, everyday interactions. This heightened awareness of my professional role was closely tied to a sense of contentment and gratitude.

Mindfulness is closely linked to the mindset that everything is allowed to be as it is. Yet alongside this acceptance was my desire for change. To embark on a journey of change, one must first know where they stand, and only then, where the journey should lead. So, where did I stand at that moment, and how did I feel about it? For the most part, I could only answer "good" to this question. I had lived a blessed life so far—there was no doubt about that. But looking more closely, I realized it wasn't all black and white, there were many shades of gray. And it was equally true that there were some gray areas. These were small points, yet perhaps decisive in determining whether I was on the right path to finding my purpose.

My life was blessed, and for that, I was grateful. Yet a certain monotony had crept into my daily life, and I often felt that something essential was missing within the structured routine. There was a certain dissatisfaction with the outer framework of my daily life. But I also felt dissatisfaction within my inner framework. In some ways, I felt dissatisfied with myself and the way I was living. My entire approach to life had strayed a bit off course. I had become overly preoccupied with external matters—practical concerns like nutrition, the house, and finances. For years, I'd hoped to win the lottery, which, of course, never happened. The diagnosis and the looming threat of death allowed me to reorient my thinking in a more meaningful direction. In the face of death, what I owned or could own—whether material things or social status—felt meaningless. I felt no desire to achieve more in these areas in the time I had left.

Dissatisfaction requires the knowledge—or at least the belief—that something better exists. The various aspects of possession did not satisfy my thirst for life in the face of death. Of course, the reassurance of having a financial safety net was comforting, as the various treatment options all cost money. For that, too, I was grateful, since only through financial security could I pursue certain therapeutic paths. Yet money was merely a means to an end—health—and health, in turn, a medium for living a meaningful life. It's not money that fulfills us but, as theologian and philosopher Paul Tillich called them, our "ultimate concerns." So, what were my ultimate concerns? What truly fulfilled me? There are undoubtedly many answers to this, but for me, one of the most important was: connection. Connection with myself, with other people, with the world around me, and with God.

By "connection," I mean genuine connection—being mindful, present, and fully aware. As I mentioned, I had neglected my connection with myself in recent years. One reason for this was my lack of awareness of this deep need; it was masked by the demands of daily life. At times, I sensed this need, but the distractions of everyday life made it easy to ignore. The threat of death brought this need to the surface; I could feel it clearly and no longer wished to ignore it.

In recent years, I had often thought that external conditions were why I couldn't pursue many things important to me. Now I found that by changing my inner framework, the external framework shifted as well. By giving greater priority to my connection with myself, I was able to make small yet meaningful changes in my everyday life. From the outside, they seemed like small adjustments, but internally, they made a noticeable difference. For instance, I stopped going to the canteen during my 30-minute lunch break at work, primarily because the food there didn't align with my diet. Instead, I used that time to take a 20-30 minute walk alone in a small park. This time—in connection with myself and nature—made a subtle yet significant difference. It was qualitatively far more valuable than a hot meal in the canteen. At home, I made it part of my routine to take at least a 30-minute walk alone each day. During this time, I could focus entirely on myself—my thoughts and my feelings.

Walking is an activity that deepens my connection with myself. This connection came easily and felt deeply natural. It's easy to see why walking was so important to many thinkers, like Immanuel Kant. Many of the key thoughts and reflections in this book arose during my walks. As I walked, thoughts, impressions, memories, desires, and longings flowed in and out. As Carl Zuckmayer put it: "The beginning of thought, free and independent thinking, the vigilant tracking of unexpected mental paths, works best when the body is in motion."

In addition to my walks, I began taking a few moments almost every evening—while Julia was putting our youngest to bed—to retreat to our bedroom, sit quietly, connect with myself, and pray. I'm not sure what to call it—whether meditation, contemplation, or prayer—but in this case, the label doesn't matter to me. What mattered was a mindful connection with myself and with God, even though it was often difficult.

A crucial step for me was also the decision to bring this book into being. I took some time each evening to write this book. This book is part of my journey to encounter and engage with myself. It conveys my personal experiences and reflections, and this act of expression alone is fulfilling and meaningful to me. Writing helps me organize my thoughts. Writing gives my thoughts meaningful structure and coherence. Certain insights emerged only through the process of writing. My thoughts, however, are not purely my own creation; my mind unconsciously draws on countless intellectual influences that have shaped my thinking and attitudes over the past 30 years. These influences stem primarily from books on religion and spirituality, existential philosophy, and humanistic-existential psychotherapy. Karl Jaspers, Irvin Yalom, Viktor Frankl, and Paul Tillich have been especially influential to me. Many other important influences—from authors of countless books and encounters with people—cannot be listed, as they are too numerous and often no longer conscious to me. I have absorbed their thoughts and ideas, internalized them, and they've become a part of me. Thus, this book reflects not only my connection with myself but also my connection with others. It is also sustained by the hope of building a connection with others, that readers may be touched and perhaps even changed by some of these thoughts.

One of the most formative books for me was perhaps *Words of Love: Answers to Young People's Questions on Love and Sexuality* by Majerus Mill (I had to Google the title and author to recall them). At fourteen, I was searching for guidance, and this book profoundly shaped my views on love and sexuality. I'm not sure how I would judge the book today, but as a teenager, it was invaluable and formative for me. The idea of love as an ideal, rather than its erotic-sexual reflection, became a central motif in my life. From my own experience, I can affirm that books hold the power to shape life paths.

The first book (or rather, booklet), which I wrote during my student years, was titled *The Way of Love in the Shadow of Anxiety*. I still vividly remember that time, filled with insights about love and anxiety, gathering them and bringing them into a meaningful context. Whether or not the booklet would be published was secondary; the act of writing itself brought me joy and fulfillment. Writing this current book allowed me to reconnect with that experience.

This book symbolizes the inseparable unity between my connection with myself and my dependence on connection with others. It holds my thoughts and reflections, yet these were shaped and inspired by others. I need others to know myself and to receive essential impulses for my becoming. Our thoughts often go in circles; new insights and growth require external impulses. Our inner self requires inspiration to grow and flourish, just as plants need water.

So, how was my connection with other people in my life, and how did the threat of death change that? Social relationships have always been somewhat ambivalent for me, and the threat of death didn't change that much. At times, encounters and genuine connections with others came easily. In those encounters, self-disclosure felt effortless, and meaningful conversations developed naturally, touching and enriching me. Such deep encounters were like a life elixir for me and a central reason for my choice to become a psychotherapist. I never regretted those moments of deep human connection—when the masks fell, when we could reveal our vulnerability and be truly understood and accepted. I always felt fulfilled after such conversations.

In my current daily life, such encounters are rarer than I would like. Deep, genuine encounters require an environment marked by safety, intimacy, personal openness, and the right timing. Such an environment is often unavailable in everyday life. Moreover, such deep encounters are the bright moments of our lives, and we likely can't dwell in them continuously—just as we can't remain in blazing sunlight for long. It would exhaust us. Thus, superficial encounters are also part of life's natural flow.

Regrettably, I often didn't feel comfortable in these superficial encounters, which reflected another side of the truth. On one hand, I lived for human connection, but on the other, I had always been socially anxious and often preferred to avoid social activities. I felt selectively insecure and uncomfortable in groups and large crowds, especially when speaking in front of many people. This hasn't changed, though I've learned to handle it "professionally," so most people likely don't notice. Small talk was never my strength either. Not because I felt above it. Beyond my insecurity, I often simply didn't have much to say on many topics. For instance, I didn't read the newspaper or keep up with the news. On the one hand, I had lost trust in the media due to various experiences; on the other, I didn't want to burden myself with predominantly negative news. My unfamiliarity with current political and social issues significantly limited my available conversation topics. In addition, I had long tried to follow Socrates' "three sieves":

A man approached the wise Socrates and said, "Listen, Socrates, I must tell you something!" Socrates interrupted him, saying: "Wait! Have you sifted what you want to tell me through the three sieves?" Surprised, the man asked: "Three sieves? What three sieves?" Socrates explained, "Let's see if what you want to share passes through the three sieves. The first sieve is truth. Are you certain that what you want to share is true?" The man answered, "No, I just heard it from someone." Socrates replied, "Then it must pass through the second sieve, goodness. Is it something good that you want to share?" The man replied hesitantly, "No, not really. Quite the opposite." Socrates continued, "Then only the third sieve remains: necessity. Is it truly necessary to share what's troubling you?" The man responded, "No, it's not really necessary." Socrates smiled and said, "Well, if the story you want to share is neither true, good, nor necessary, then forget it and spare me from it."

Yet applying these three sieves in everyday life quickly cuts many conversations short. I was never as bold or consistent as Socrates in interrupting my conversation partners with the three sieves, but inwardly, I disengaged if I felt the content didn't pass through them.

My way of life often didn't align with society's common customs. My interests and beliefs often differed from those of the majority around me, and many activities others enjoyed brought me little pleasure. I didn't enjoy fairs, beer tents, dance events, parties, or carnival parades. I wasn't involved in clubs or organizations. My religious beliefs were fundamentally Christian, though unorthodox and shaped by various influences, and from a Catholic perspective, heretical. I was skeptical of infant baptism, communion, and confirmation, which rendered me unfit to be a godparent. I often felt unable to meet social expectations, and at times, I simply didn't want to. My social life certainly wasn't helped by the fact that I often got lost in thought and forgot about social activities. I rarely stayed in touch with friends and frequently forgot important anniversaries. Fortunately, most of my friends were forgiving.

What had changed in my relationships because of the diagnosis and the looming threat of death? Not dramatically so. However, there were small changes—some leading to deeper connection, others to greater distance.

As I mentioned earlier, I often felt that the inner gap between myself and those around me had widened. The "healthy" lived in a different inner reality than I did. I often felt as though I was in a liminal space—still connected to the normal life of productivity and achievement, yet detached from those values, which now seemed secondary to me. The material world had grown somewhat irrelevant to me.

My approach to treating the cancer wasn't conventional; more than once, my oncologists let me know that while they tolerated my path, they didn't fully approve of it. Here, too, I stood outside the role of the good patient who obediently follows doctors' recommendations, instead becoming an outlier who followed his own path. I often felt vulnerable and fragile, reluctant to expose myself and my beliefs to public judgment. As a result, I usually avoided talking about my illness. I also felt that talking too much about it would somehow solidify the disease, giving it more space than I wished. I also didn't want to be the center of attention or receive pity. All in all, there were many reasons why I usually kept my illness shrouded in silence. Without a specific reason, my answer to how I was doing was a simple "so far so good," which wasn't a lie but also not the whole truth.

At the same time, the illness had become a central issue for me, one that couldn't just be brushed aside. Yalom once said of group therapy, "If an important issue is avoided in a session, then nothing essential gets discussed in that session." Perhaps this insight also applies, in a way, to everyday encounters. I found that deeper conversations usually only emerged when my illness was openly addressed first.

My relationship with groups continued to be difficult. I felt even less at ease in groups than I had before the diagnosis. Because of my strict dietary restrictions, even simple plans to eat together became complicated, and my cancer diagnosis inevitably came up whenever questions about my diet arose. The time I spent in groups was rarely fulfilling, and I often wished I could spend it differently. As a result, I avoided groups and social events even more than I had before.

On the other hand, my diagnosis made me part of an underground community. I now belonged to the community of the ill and those acutely threatened by death. Many in this group live outside the realm of healthy society, largely invisible to those who are well. The community of the ill barely exists in the daily lives of the healthy—they know it only from a distance, through stories. For healthy people, the presence of the ill is often difficult to bear, either because they feel helpless and at a loss for words or because they fear being too deeply affected or infected by suffering. The ill, in turn, no longer participate in the healthy world's daily life of work, productivity, sports, and carefree enjoyment. To the ill, the busy pursuits of the healthy can sometimes seem absurd, perhaps even laughable, in light of the tasks and goals that consume and preoccupy them.

The community of the ill was vast and diverse, including both the unknown and the famous, the poor and the rich, the educated and uneducated. The looming threat of death made us all equal, stripping away our ranks, names, and wealth, as all of it was meaningless in the face of death. We were all simply humans, confronted with the existential realities of our being, sharing similar experiences, needs, desires, and questions. I increasingly read books by people with serious illnesses, labeled "incurable" by medicine. I often saw myself in their stories and experiences, felt inspired by their thoughts, and touched by their courage, strength, and mental agility. Through their books, I felt a deep connection and sense of belonging with these people. Through the books, I could connect with their thoughts and engage in a kind of dialogue with them. What initially connected us was the shared experience of severe illness and the looming threat of death, our efforts toward healing, the search for meaning in suffering, and the preservation of human dignity, even in the face of failure.

These experiences fostered a deeper empathy for my patients. I grew to understand more deeply what it meant to be seriously ill and face the possibility of death. This enriched my ability to understand my patients, leading to deeper and more authentic relationships. I was no longer afraid of being too affected by their harrowing experiences of suffering and pain, as I was already in the midst of it myself. I believe this was valuable for everyone involved and made therapy sessions meaningful, even if nothing else was accomplished. I am also firmly convinced that it contributed to more meaningful therapy sessions.

In light of my limited time, I felt a strong desire for as many genuine, honest, and profound encounters as possible. One challenge for me was finding a balance between preserving my core self and embracing the need for change and courage to grow. It wasn't in my nature, nor my desire, to become a "group person." My wish was for personal, one-on-one encounters. Such encounters are typically only possible under certain conditions and if the other person is open to them. It was therefore important for me to protect myself, set clear boundaries, and be selective; I didn't need to connect with everyone. At the same time, I recognized that there were internal obstacles that made connecting with others difficult for me. These needed to be recognized and overcome.

One of these obstacles was a lack of mindfulness in daily life, and since my diagnosis, cultivating greater mindfulness had become central to my healing. Increasing mindfulness enriched all my relationships. My relationship with Julia had always been deep and fulfilling, full of joy and love. However, it would be dishonest to claim that over our 15 years of marriage and raising three children, with all the associated tasks and responsibilities, a certain monotony hadn't crept in. At times, it felt more like we were living side by side than truly together. The awareness, sharpened by my diagnosis, of our limited future together made our time more precious. It heightened our awareness and led to a renewed effort to make the most of our time together, which meant consciously setting aside time as a couple, to connect mindfully and be fully present with each other. We made an effort to prioritize this quality time as a couple, finding and making use of available time slots. We realized that there were, in fact, some offers of support from family and friends that we had previously been hesitant to accept. We now actively tried to take advantage of these, and while they weren't long breaks, they were enough for a hike, a sauna visit, or a concert together for a few hours. Or simply to take the time in the evening to sit together by candlelight, with a good glass of wine and our favorite music, letting genuine encounter unfold.

Yet it was sobering to realize how fragile these changes were and how quickly we could slip back into side-by-side time. Since I was mostly well in daily life, there was little to remind us of my illness and the threat to our future together. It was easy for us to forget about it. Before long, there were evenings, just like before I got sick, when we sat on opposite sides of the couch, each engaged in our own activities, without any meaningful exchange. At times, this even suited me, as my evenings were limited—between dinner, putting the kids to bed, time for prayer, working on my book, reading for new inspiration and nourishment for my soul, or managing my illness and treatment options. Evenings were often too short, and I was frequently torn between the desire to connect with Julia and the need for time for other things.

Thus, I can well understand Arthur Frank, who, after recovering from a severe illness, wrote that he feared forgetting what it was like to have been sick. Serious illness reveals what is truly important in life and can initiate many meaningful changes. Yet these valuable insights and changes are at risk as soon as we recover, as the busyness of everyday life returns and society's common values once again become omnipresent. Though my body harbored a severe, life-threatening illness at its core, I appeared healthy and fit on the outside. To hold onto these positive changes, I had to continually remind myself that my life was under acute threat.

I therefore made an effort to cultivate greater mindfulness in my encounters with myself and others. This made me more attuned to my own thoughts, feelings, and sensations, and I tried to allow them to be as they were, expressing them openly. I realized it was often difficult for me to express my feelings openly and honestly, as I held a deep-seated belief that I wasn't right as I was—that my feelings and desires lacked legitimacy. Increased mindfulness heightened my awareness of sore spots, rooted in my life history, which represented another significant obstacle to genuine connection with myself and others. After all, if you can't show kindness to yourself, how can you genuinely be kind to others?

How can you show kindness to yourself when you believe that you aren't right as you are? Even now, I found it hard to take sick leave, despite facing a deadly illness and an essential treatment that couldn't fit into a full-time work schedule. Despite everything, I felt I didn't truly have the right to take time for myself and felt the need to justify it with plausible explanations.

The root of these sore spots lay in my childhood. Though I had confronted these issues several times, they still hadn't fully healed—perhaps they never will, and perhaps that isn't even necessary. If they occasionally hurt but don't undermine my sense of connection, I can live with it. However, certain situations still triggered inappropriate emotions in me, sometimes negatively affecting my relationships. As a result, I sought support from a colleague to explore what was at play in these situations and what changes I still needed to make on my part.

Early on, my therapist reflected back to me a simple but healing impulse: I deserve this. I have the right to ask for things for myself and to carve out my own freedom. Lately, I often felt my freedom was suffocated by responsibility—that I couldn't find personal freedom amid my self-imposed obligations as a father and partner without failing in these roles. Freedom and connection became rivals. Yet freedom remained another essential lifeblood for me. My inner beliefs and values were at odds with each other.

This was compounded by the ongoing tension between freedom and security. I had often discussed this irresolvable conflict—our striving for both security and freedom—with my patients. But now, like my patients, I too was grappling with this existential conflict. As a father, the pursuit of security took on more weight—at the expense of my freedom. On a more personal, deeper level, my need for security had always held me back in life. The musician Passenger aptly expresses this in his song Wrong Direction: "I'd love to feel love but I can't stand the rejection. I hide behind my jokes as a form of protection." Hiding is a way to shield oneself from rejection. Time and again, I hid my true thoughts and feelings behind a wall of reserve, caution, or superficiality. In this way, I was safe, but not free—and not truly connected. Even with Julia, I wasn't always completely honest, as I avoided conflict and longed for harmony. Deep down, I knew that true love requires speaking up about uncomfortable and painful things when they matter. Still, it remains difficult to put into practice what we already understand.

Every human being is a "person." The word person is derived from "per" (meaning "through") and "sonare" (meaning "to sound"). Thus, a person is something that "resonates through the mask." Socrates once said, "Speak, that I may see you!" What makes a person truly human is invisible to the eyes. It becomes visible only when a person communicates, revealing their inner self through speech. If we don't speak openly and honestly about what moves us—our thoughts and feelings—we cannot truly be recognized as a person. I may have social relationships, but in those connections, I am not present as my true self; I am merely an outer shell. I might say something, but what I say doesn't reflect my true self—it's only words I believe my counterpart wants to hear, or words that fit a specific social role. If I don't dare to reveal myself, I am not truly present in these relationships, and it's not me who is appreciated and liked by my friend, but merely my role and outer appearance. In such relationships, I cannot experience genuine connection.

What could be worse than never experiencing true connection, than never truly being known by anyone because I never dared to leave my fortress—and ultimately, dying alone? To be recognized and loved as a person, I must take the risk of self-revelation. Coming to terms with death can help me do that. If I can face, accept, and even welcome death, won't all other fears lose their terror? What harm is there, then, if someone finds me odd or doesn't understand my beliefs and way of life? In the face of death, what truly matters is being at peace with myself and with my God. Confronting and accepting inevitable death can render me invulnerable to the world's threats. Accepting death can strengthen my courage to reveal myself to the world and achieve real connection. I must dare to do it today, as I don't know if I'll have the chance tomorrow. On the other hand, it is precisely the connection with a loved one that can lead us to fear death and refuse to accept it, as death means separation from the beloved. We, as humans, may never escape the unresolved contradictions of life.

The heroic tale of Achilles can be interpreted in this way. The basic outline of the story can be quickly summarized. According to legend, Achilles is dipped into the underworld river Styx by his mother, Thetis, a sea nymph and daughter of the sea god Nereus, making Achilles invulnerable. Only his heel, where his mother held him, was untouched by the water and remained vulnerable. Achilles grows to become the bravest of all Greek heroes. The

Trojan War is won only with his help, but Achilles also meets his death when an arrow strikes his vulnerable heel. The exact circumstances of Achilles' death differ across accounts, with some saying Achilles had fallen in love and met his end as he sought the hand of his beloved.

How can we interpret this story in relation to our own lives? Achilles becomes invulnerable when immersed in the Styx. In Greek mythology, the Styx symbolizes the boundary between the world of the living and the realm of the dead. At this boundary, one is no longer fully in the world of the living, yet not entirely in the realm of the dead. This often reflects the experience of those confronted with serious illness and threatened by death—not fully alive, yet not dead. The Styx can symbolically represent this boundary experience. What anchors Achilles in this boundary experience is the love and care of his mother. At the same time, this loving bond creates his weak point, leaving him vulnerable. After this boundary experience, Achilles reconciles with death, loses his fear of death and loss, and thus becomes "invulnerable" to the threats of the material world. He transforms into the bravest hero. Yet he becomes vulnerable again when he falls in love, reconnecting with the material world. Love brings vulnerability when we fear the loss of a loved one. Through love, Achilles once again faces worry and fear, and death—the inevitable separation from the beloved—regains its terror.

Deep connection often arises only through the courage to reveal oneself fully, in all one's vulnerability. This means being able to reveal everything to the other person—even those parts we deem bad or wrong, the things we're ashamed of and judge ourselves for. Nothing is more liberating and healing than discovering that even these parts can be accepted—and perhaps even loved—by another person. However, it takes courage to take the first step of self-revelation. Confronting my mortality can help me do this. The death that stands at the door reminds me that I will never achieve perfection—and that I don't have to. The way I am today must be good enough, despite flaws and all. I don't need to be perfect—just true to myself. It's about radical self-acceptance, about generosity and compassion, even toward oneself.

A central theme of my alternative therapy approach involves examining whether life is experienced as fulfilling. The goal is to identify and remove all obstacles to personal happiness and to do everything possible to lead a fulfilling life. My initial assessment of this issue was that I probably didn't need much action here. My rational mind told me I lived a privileged life for which I should feel grateful and content. But I also knew the question reached deeper—it wasn't just about a rational attitude and evaluation, but about feelings and positive energy. Did I find joy in my life? Did I look forward to each day when I got up in the morning? I had to answer no. I felt more lethargic, took longer to get going in the morning, and found many daily activities required effort.

I was unsure whether this was because I gave too little room to my true desires, inclinations, and needs, or if it was simply that my body's burdens were draining my energy. I often lacked energy for everything—even activities I enjoyed were approached half-heartedly, as I remained in "economy mode." Today, I believe that both play a role. Changing my diet gave me more energy, and that alone made my life feel livelier, with more ease and joy. Yet I still felt as if I had strayed from my life's path. What fulfilled and defined me was somewhat absent from my current life. At the same time, I needed to first figure out what truly mattered. Fortunate is the person who knows what fulfills their life and can dedicate themselves to it.

I had to acknowledge that this question was indeed relevant to my healing journey. At the same time, I struggled with the idea of "pursuing happiness." Of course, I wanted to be happy too, but my profession had taught me that happiness is a complex concept with paradoxical qualities. Research on happiness shows that the more one pursues happiness, the more likely they are to become unhappy. Directly pursuing happiness is not an effective path to fulfillment. It is better to follow the advice of Danish philosopher Søren Kierkegaard, who said that the door to happiness opens backward; to enter, you must first step back.

I view happiness similarly to health: positive and desirable in principle, but not the highest good. In fact, I view the tendency to elevate these two as the highest values with a critical eye and prefer not to go down that path. When personal happiness becomes the highest measure of value, I believe it entails significant risks, such as indulging one's own desires and needs at the expense of essential values and relationships.

To me, gratitude, mindfulness, connectedness, and finding and fulfilling one's purpose are far more important than the pursuit of happiness. Knowing what matters most to me, realigning my life toward it, and striving to fulfill it. From this arise positive visions and energies. Or as Viktor E. Frankl put it: A person doesn't seek happiness itself, but rather a reason to be happy.

Ultimately, it's less about the question of happiness and more about the question of life's meaning for me. Meaning is tied to the direction of one's life, to choosing and walking a certain path. And here I return to the beginning of the chapter, where I questioned whether I had strayed from my life's path, whether I was in danger of missing life's meaning.

What answers have I found so far to the question of what matters most, of what my path and purpose are? Naturally, the answers to this question are manifold; I haven't found them all, and I can't express all the ones I have. It's not that I totally lacked significant answers before the illness. Over time, some essential things had simply been lost—or perhaps not lost, but merely pushed into the background. Looking back on my life's path and searching for meaningful moments, I can discover recurring themes that emerge in this chapter.

Since my youth, I've always felt a deep yearning for genuine connection and true love. The bright moments in which I was fortunate to experience this had the power to steer my life toward a therapeutic profession. This inspired a lasting effort to become a compassionate and loving person. My family is a gift rooted in these experiences.

As a young adult, I discovered the healing power of consciously spending time alone, especially while wandering in nature. Deeply hurt by unrequited love, I took a solo trip to Merano, where I hiked, read Hermann Hesse, and allowed myself time for reflection. When I returned, a sense of openness and brightness about my future had come back, and the wounds began to heal. Since then, the motif of the pilgrim has become part of my identity—journeying with myself, free and unbound, seeking connection and healing, but also learning to endure solitude.

Starting my studies and moving to Trier felt like the beginning of my real life—the discovery of my "intellectual home." I ventured alone into a new world. The chance to freely develop my inclinations, to meet kindred spirits, and to affirm my own intellectual abilities brought me joy and fulfillment. There was room and nourishment for my desire to delve deeply into philosophical, psychological, and spiritual subjects. I also discovered the joy that comes from writing a book.

Today, I have a clearer sense of who I truly am—and who I am not. Productivity and action are not my primary sources of fulfillment. In my childhood and youth, I was a dreamer who simply wanted to play. I had little interest in work or manual labor, which meant I never quite fit into my family, who had run a small crafts business in a village for generations. I was the odd one out—the "softie" who preferred to avoid practical tasks. Over time, my interests and talents began to emerge in sports, the natural sciences, music, religion, and philosophy—subjects that held little importance in my family. I can still hear my grandmother dismissing any profession ending with "-logy" as insignificant. Still, this didn't stop me from studying psychology. Over time, I tried to bridge the gap by aligning myself, at least somewhat, with my family's values. I completed a craft apprenticeship with good results and developed an interest in various manual tasks. Together with Julia, I bought an old house and took on most of the renovation work myself. I tried to keep our home in good condition and spent a lot of time focused on it. But I could only meet these expectations to a limited extent and eventually realized that one can't walk multiple paths at once. As a result, I lacked time for what truly mattered: reading spiritual, philosophical, and psychological books, wandering and reflecting, dreaming, and engaging with others on these topics. Since my diagnosis, I've been rediscovering my true self. While I still deeply value craftsmanship and even plan to build a drum set for one of my sons, I now understand that my essence lies elsewhere.

So, I don't believe it's about finding new purposes for myself. Instead, it's about giving more space to the central themes of my life. I want to embrace my true interests and inclinations again, without postponing them for an uncertain future. Some days, I'm certain I'm on the right path, but then doubts arise again. In the end, the opposites that shape my life persist. The looming threat of death still shakes me—evoking fear and anxiety, reminding me of my doubts, and confronting me with helplessness; yet it also wakes me up, makes me feel alive, and gives me courage. It forces me to let go, yet also to hold on to what matters most. I seek deep connection with others, yet I also need the freedom to be alone with myself. Perhaps the key to fulfillment and healing lies in balancing these opposing forces within.

So, I haven't reached the destination yet. I haven't fully become the person I'm meant to be; I'm still in the process of becoming. I believe it's part of human nature to always be on a journey —our essence is that of being in motion, and to be human is to continuously become. My self-actualization remains a continual task. The imminent threat of death has shaken me awake, showing me that I need to walk my path consciously—with clear direction and a focus on the essentials in life. And that I need to walk my path today, not put it off until tomorrow.

Death is the star guiding the traveler on life's path. Only death lends urgency to our actions and helps us recognize the value of life. In the face of death, what remains essential are the truly important things in life. Therefore, it's essential not to repress the thought of death but to keep it alive in our awareness. In this sense, Arthur Frank (10), who was also diagnosed with cancer, writes: "As long as life remains a recovery, I try to seize the life I someday want to have lived. The value of remaining a person with cancer is to keep asking the question: If I get sick again, what will I tell myself about the way I spent my time? ... When I feel I have no time to walk out and watch the sunlight on the river, my recovery has gone too far."

Healing and Spirituality

When I speak of spirituality, its meaning may initially seem unclear. Spirituality is a term that is frequently used but difficult to grasp. No universally accepted definition exists. Therefore, I should briefly outline what I personally understand by spirituality. The word "spirituality" originates from the Latin term spiritus, meaning spirit, breath, or essence. To me, spirituality is deeply connected to the "divine spirit"—a lived faith and an active relationship with the divine foundation of all existence. Some perspectives on spirituality set aside the concept of God, focusing instead on practices that cultivate mental calm, concentration, mindfulness, and compassion. While I find these qualities positive and valuable, without the divine element, I can only view such spiritual practices as meaningful exercises for life rather than as true spirituality. For me, spirituality is deeply tied to connectedness—something that many experts also consider the core of spirituality. At its core lies my connection with God. Since God is the source of all existence, this connection extends to other people, all living beings, the entire world, and to myself. For me, spirituality inherently involves a reference to the dimension of time—acknowledging where we come from and where we are going. The great spiritual traditions express our origins through creation myths and are grounded in a legacy of personal experiences of the divine. In many spiritual traditions, the finiteness of human life holds a central place—particularly the themes of death and what may follow. Buddha described meditation on death as the royal path. In the Christian tradition, the phrase "memento mori" ("remember that you will die") became a well-known tool for living rightly, even amid varying interpretations of what "right" means.

Writing a chapter on spirituality is not without its challenges. I have neither a theological education nor am I a spiritual teacher. I want to emphasize that what follows is neither official doctrine nor a guide to spiritual development. The reflections in this chapter represent my personal thoughts and experiences along my spiritual journey. My goal is not to present a "this is the right way," but rather a "this is how I experience it, how it makes sense to me." I believe that every person who lives a religious or spiritual life can have essential experiences and thoughts that reflect an aspect of divine reality—thoughts that may touch and help others discover God in a new way and find their own path.

I root deeply in religion and spirituality. In my childhood and youth, I was deeply involved and active in our small Christian (Catholic) community, and during my youth and early adulthood, I immersed myself in the study of religion and spirituality. My focus was initially on the Christian faith, but through liberation theology, I gradually became more critical of Catholic dogma, which led me to think more independently. This journey led me to explore other world religions and to consider studying comparative religion with a focus on Buddhism, along with philosophy and psychology. However, my experiences as a conscientious objector in a psychosomatic clinic, where I had meaningful encounters with patients, shifted my path toward psychology and psychotherapy. The strongly empirical focus of my psychology studies nurtured only the rational, scientifically inclined part of my mind—analytical and driven by empirical evidence. The message of my university education was clear: an analytical approach and rational mindset were paramount. In contrast, any worldview deemed irrational or superstitious was met with derision and irony from above. Religious beliefs were included in this view, reinforcing the core message that scientific psychology and irrational religion are incompatible.

These experiences during training complicated my relationship with faith. On one hand, my faith remained strong and meaningful; on the other, my lived faith faded into the background. Inner conflicts emerged, especially in my work as a psychotherapist. I saw myself as a scientifically-minded psychologist, keen to avoid any appearance of irrationality or superstition. Additionally, there were warnings about how power dynamics between therapist and patient could easily lead to the imposition of the therapist's personal beliefs (an "ideological imposition"), as patients in a vulnerable state are especially receptive to the therapist's views. Consequently, I made a conscious effort to keep religion and spirituality out of my therapeutic conversations with patients. I felt uneasy whenever religious or spiritual topics arose in therapy sessions, as though I were stepping onto forbidden ground. Inner conflicts also surfaced in my personal spiritual life. My faith remained, yet I was no longer actively practicing it. I stopped attending church as a young man because the Mass gave me little, and certain dogmatic teachings and rituals put me off. Yet I missed the personal reflection in prayer, which had also lost its place in my daily life. It had slipped far down my list of priorities, and I convinced myself I simply didn't have the time. Today, I have to admit that the real issue wasn't a lack of time but an inner conflict. Whenever I expressed personal religious beliefs or withdrew to pray, I felt vulnerable and exposed, as if stepping into territory my professional authorities ridiculed. One of my personal and professional role models has been the renowned American psychotherapist and author Irvin Yalom. In several books, he writes that he is completely non-religious, and he emphasizes that, in his view, religiosity is ultimately just a defense against the fear of death. To me, this implies that religiosity is merely a crutch for those too weak to face the harsh realities of life directly. This made it even more challenging to establish a natural relationship with my spirituality. Although I held a different view from Yalom on this point, his influence undoubtedly lingered in the background.

Belief in God and in a connection between God and humanity struggles today in a scientifically materialistic world. Believing in things without scientific explanation or material basis is challenging for us. Even the concept of "free will" comes into question, as the brain provides the material basis for will—in a scientifically determined material world, there is no freedom. In the material world, there is only cause and effect, not free choice. Yet this contradicts our immediate sense of freedom, especially when moral demands are placed upon us and we wrestle with decisions.

Connection with God is likewise a spiritual reality without material foundation, making it challenging for our empirically oriented minds to grasp. What kind of connection could transcend mere (wishful) thinking? Modern quantum physics supports my belief that such connectedness may not be mere wishful thinking but could also have a place within science. In quantum physics, for instance, there are so-called entangled particles, sharing a connection that defies traditional concepts of local reality. Entangled particles are linked by properties like polarization or spin; a measurement or change in one particle instantly affects the other, regardless of the distance between them—even if they move in opposite directions at light speed. This type of connection between entangled particles appears to be proven, commonly referred to as "spooky action at a distance." Yet a satisfying explanation for how this connection works remains elusive; after all, it would require an interaction faster than the speed of light, which is impossible according to current physics. For me, the lack of explanation isn't important; what matters is that such an immaterial connection exists. Perhaps, at an elemental level, we are all entangled with all of existence. A connection to God and all existence need not be created; it already exists.

In quantum physics, matter can be seen as condensed light and, conversely, light as fluid matter. To me, this forms a beautiful spiritual image. Who are we? From a quantum-physical viewpoint, our material bodies consist of condensed light. Light, then, forms the foundation of our being—for me, the light of God: "And God said, Let there be light!" Interestingly, studies show that physicists are the most religious group after theologians. It appears that hard science and spirituality are not incompatible. We all belong to this material world, and yet, in some way, we do not. The ultimate questions remain unanswered, yet for me, there is a meaningful, sustaining foundation beneath all existence, which I call God. I yearn for a living connection with God, even as I exist in this material world governed by the laws of classical physics.

With the cancer diagnosis, my spiritual need reemerged with renewed urgency. It demanded greater space and time in my life—particularly a connection with God and the need for "spiritual nourishment" through reflection on spiritual themes. Each evening, I set aside a bit of time to withdraw and pray. I made space for spiritual reflection and began reading more books on these topics once again.

Deep within, I felt that returning to my spirituality was essential for my healing. For me, living in connection with God encompasses healing. Spirituality and healing have a long-shared history, yet their relationship today is strained. Throughout much of human history, they were inseparable. Healing was traditionally provided by the spiritual leaders of their time and culture—from shamans to monks. The New Testament recounts numerous healings performed by Jesus and later by his disciples. In more recent times, spiritual healers and "mediums" have emerged. However, self-proclaimed spiritual healers are not always effective, as many disappointing outcomes illustrate. The critical mindset of the modern age has led to empirical studies on spiritual healing, with results that are not always convincing. Indeed, it seems some spiritual healers are more concerned with their own gain, casting a shadow over the entire field and fueling doubt. Without rational, empirical explanations, those seeking help find it difficult to logically assess the effectiveness of healing approaches. Which spiritual healer can be trusted? Which approach is meaningful, and which is not?

There are many different approaches to "spiritual healing." In one tradition, the sick person is largely a passive recipient of "healing energy" from a spiritual healer or leader—be it through intercessory prayer, laying on of hands, receiving the Eucharist, drumming, or trance. In another approach, the sick person actively engages in their own spiritual healing—through prayer or by striving for spiritual development. However, what exactly spiritual development means is a difficult question to answer. I have no expertise in distinguishing and describing stages of spiritual development. To me, the highest form of spiritual development is enlightenment and becoming one with God. To me, spiritual development involves cultivating qualities such as a constant connection with God, trust in God, wisdom, knowledge, compassionate love for all beings, heightened presence in the here and now, peacefulness, and a balanced temperament. The path to cultivating these qualities includes spiritual practice through prayer, meditation, and daily application.

In his book Healing Words, Larry Dossey (11) summarizes numerous empirical findings on the effects of thoughts and prayers. The findings suggest that thoughts and prayers exert influence, even across time and space. For instance, experiments indicate that thoughts can influence organisms like bacteria, yeast cultures, or mice, and even affect the outcomes of a random number generator. A central focus of the book is the effect of prayer and whether it can truly bring about healing.

While reading Dossey's book, I found myself confronted with an inner conflict—on one hand, critical skepticism, and on the other, an attraction to the subject. For many years, I have been critical of traditional forms of prayer, like intercessory prayer. In this regard, I found myself aligned with Immanuel Kant, who saw it as presumptuous "to try to sway God from the plan of His wisdom (to our present advantage) through the insistent importunity of petitions." Similarly, Oscar Wilde observed, "When the gods wish to punish us, they answer our prayers."

However, I have remained very open to other forms of prayer, and I feel a deep need for them. In my early adulthood, I visited the ecumenical brotherhood led by Frère Roger in the small Burgundian village of Taizé, France, on several occasions. The brotherhood became known for its gatherings of young people from around the world and its distinctive contemplative prayers accompanied by mantra-like chants. In these contemplative prayers and chants, I felt immediately at home. This was the form of prayer that felt fundamentally right to me. My spiritual home in prayer became contemplation or devotion—an open form that follows no instructions or set words and can even be wordless. It is more about a sense of the sacred, a feeling of unity with God. The philosopher of religion, Paul Tillich (12), describes prayer as "the infinite longing of a finite being for its infinite source; the reunion with the divine ground of our being." To me, this kind of prayer is not about influencing God to achieve a desired outcome but about remaining open to the divine spirit so that it may grasp, permeate, and transform me. I do not act on God; instead, I allow myself to be acted upon by Him, trusting that whatever happens is good. Devotion is characterized by openness, acceptance, and gratitude. This form of prayer suited my nature; it simply felt right.

The scientific findings compiled in Dossey's book suggest that prayers can contribute to the healing of serious illness, though certainly not always. He distinguishes between two contrasting types of prayer: on one hand, the demanding intercessory prayer of "I ask for a specific result," and on the other, devotion as a connection with

God in gratitude and openness, trusting in "Not my will, but Thine be done." He explores whether healing is more likely to follow a fervent petition or a prayer of devotion. The scientific findings suggest that healing is more likely to occur through an undirected prayer—one that is open to any outcome rather than focused on a specific result. It appears that those who do not press for healing are more likely to experience it. Undirected prayers are not always answered, but when they are, it is invariably in a way that benefits the individual. Additional studies report similar findings. For instance, no positive effects were found for traditional intercessory prayers, whether offered by others for a sick person or by the sick person for their own health. However, positive effects were found for those who prayed when their prayers were directed toward others. In summary, one might say that prayer benefits the person praying, especially when they shift focus away from themselves and adopt an attitude of openness toward outcomes.

To me, this finding is important to avoid falling into a tendency within the spiritual scene that uncritically and one-sidedly emphasizes a positive mental attitude. There is a common belief that a patient's positive mental outlook is the decisive factor in whether healing occurs. Many self-help books, particularly in the esoteric realm, prescribe what they consider to be the right mental attitudes for healing. However, this belief is not confined to esoteric self-help books. Today, as I write these lines, I received a newsletter from a cancer clinic discussing the "healing power of the mind," claiming that this power accounts for about 80% of success in cancer healing. The author of the newsletter writes that "a strong and positive belief in healing not only reduces stress and fear but also brings life-threatening illnesses under control." What I find particularly problematic is the notion of control—the belief that cancer can be controlled through positive thinking. The conclusion is: "The mind leads, and the body follows."

To me, this conclusion is deeply problematic. This belief implies that if a person remains sick or dies, their faith must not have been strong enough, or they failed to adopt the right mindset or were too weak to maintain it consistently. Such an implication brings blame and devaluation of the ill person dangerously close. I believe healing is a complex process with many facets, influenced by numerous factors. Oversimplifications can be more harmful than helpful. I don't wish to dismiss the potential benefits of maintaining a positive attitude. There is undoubtedly power in positive thinking, and hopefulness, along with trust in a positive future and meaningful life goals, can be healing. However, I resist these simplifications and the implications they carry. To me, they reflect a form of human hubris—the notion that the world is controllable and that we alone are masters of our health. An active spirituality positively influences our health, but it does not guarantee it. There are saints who are sick and sinners who are healthy. Dossey's findings cast doubt on the esoteric tendency to claim that healing primarily relies on a mind centered on positive affirmations. It seems to me that the paradox is that the best way to achieve goals in spiritual practice is to let go of them. The best mental attitude appears to be one of connection with God, marked by openness, trust, gratitude, and "Thy will be done."

These insights and reflections encouraged me to continue and deepen my path of devotion and contemplation. Striving for genuine acceptance of all possible outcomes has become a central task on my healing journey, one I practice daily. Sometimes, it comes naturally, and I feel genuinely open, even to what might be seen as an undesirable outcome for my cancer. At other times, I feel inner resistance and notice that my acceptance is only superficial, subtly driven by the hidden wish that it might lead to my desired outcome. The mind is subtle and cunning. Sometimes, I chastise myself for this; on better days, I meet myself with compassion and understanding, recognizing that this tendency to "cling to life at all costs" is simply human.

Daily prayer has once again become an integral part of my routine. I miss it when I don't find time to pray—whether because the day was too packed or I couldn't summon the energy. In prayer, my faith feels alive; without regular prayer, it becomes lukewarm and powerless, fading into the background of my worldly life. I have always resonated with Paul Tillich's view of "prayer as the fundamental act of faith" and its inherent connection to love. My understanding is that Jesus taught us the essence of the Christian faith is actually simple: the entire religious framework is based on the double commandment of love—to love God with all one's heart and to love one's neighbor as oneself. Yet the question of what love truly is remains exceedingly difficult to answer. There are various answers to this—some complementary, others conflicting. Martin Buber's definition—Love is the responsibility of an I for a Thou—seems to me a down-to-earth and pragmatic answer, carrying a strong call to action. In contrast, Paul Tillich's definition offers a more abstract, spiritual perspective: Love is the reunion of that which inherently belongs together. Thus, if prayer is about reuniting with the divine ground of our being, then it becomes a fundamental act of loving God, the fundamental act of faith.

In prayer, I deliberately make time for communion with God. This connection doesn't need to be established; it is always present. Yet I am not always aware of it. Even when I make time for it, I don't always perceive the connection consciously. For me, it's a matter of mindfulness. Just as it's challenging for me to stay consciously connected to myself for more than a few seconds before my thoughts drift to the past or future—even though this connection to myself is always present—so it is with my connection to God. My practice in devotion is to remain mindful, to be attuned, and to stay open to being touched by God's spirit. From this connection, I draw strength, energy, trust, hope, gratitude, peace, joy, compassion, and healing. After prayer, I return to daily life with a greater sense of openness and loving attentiveness. Still, I struggle to sustain these qualities throughout the day. Sometimes, I feel as though I'm still at the very beginning of my journey, as the effects of prayer quickly fade, and I'm repeatedly drawn into the small distractions of daily life, pushing the essential into the background.

Reflecting on what I've written, I would say that spiritual development and prayer often support physical recovery or, in some cases, even lead to complete healing. Such complete healings are often termed "spontaneous remissions," regarded as "miracles" or "random events" because medical science lacks an explanation for them. I'd be lying if I said I didn't wish for such a complete healing. I want to live and remain a part of this world. I do everything within my power to regain health or at least to live as long and as fully as possible.

In recent months, I've read several books on spiritual healing, and in many, physical healing seemed to be the central focus. Yet all healing is temporary—merely a postponement, a gift of a little more time. Ultimately, we cannot escape death. Severe illness and the confrontation with death ought to teach us not to cling desperately to life but to live well, so that we may die well. As Hermann Hesse wrote, "So then, heart, take leave and heal!"

Thus, physical health is not the ultimate measure of success in my healing. I wish for health, but ultimately, it is secondary to living a fulfilled existence. If the illness disappears, I will be deeply grateful. However, if it does not, there are still plenty of reasons for a fulfilled existence and therefore for gratitude. I believe there are always reasons to be thankful. And when I am grateful, I also feel happy.

At times, I'm surprised by how sustaining my faith has proven to be in the face of my cancer diagnosis, despite how much I have neglected my religious life in recent years. My belief in the sustaining ground of God's reality gives me deep trust that things will turn out good, regardless of how my cancer ultimately unfolds. Of course, I also experience doubt, and there are days when I have a clear idea of what a "good" outcome might look like, directing my desires and longings toward God. Yet when I reflect deeply and remember that my life journey is ultimately finite, I feel a powerful acceptance of this reality. We come from God, and to Him we return. In a way, it's a beautiful thought, even if the idea of leaving this world is painful. And I hope that the path to that final moment will not be marked by too much pain or deprivation. Often, my fears concern less the fact of death and more the how of it.

I also find humility and courage in the example of Jesus Christ. Reflecting on my situation and wrestling with how young I still am, thinking of all I could still do, I realized how young Jesus was when He was crucified, with His life still open and so much left to accomplish. He surely knew what was coming—He understood the pain, humiliation, and suffering that lay ahead. It was a relief to realize that even Jesus was shaken by the prospect of His suffering and asked God to let the cup pass from Him. Jesus could easily have saved Himself and avoided His tragic fate. Yet He trusted in God: "Not my will, but Yours be done," trusting that God's will would be good. Jesus' life is a testament that it's not the length of life that matters, but its meaning and fullness. Considering such reflections, can I truly struggle with my own fate? Instead, I want to take Jesus as my example and place my trust in God. I don't wish to resist my fate but to channel my strength toward following the call of life, focusing on what is essential, and accomplishing as much as I can. Perhaps my path is to survive this cancer—or perhaps it is to face death with dignity and courage. If even someone like Jesus had to die so young and painfully, then perhaps I can accept this possible fate more easily.

Many extraordinary people, through the way they accepted fate and death with trust in God, have become shining examples to me. I feel deep compassion for them and would feel honored in their company if I prove myself worthy. Names such as Dietrich Bonhoeffer and Etty Hillesum come to mind. For them, too, trust in God was a solid foundation, along with the conviction that there are more important things than mere survival.

My emotional state isn't always steady. Some days, it's easier for me to accept my illness and feel optimistic. On other days, I struggle more with my illness. During those times, I feel burdened by implicit questions arising from esoteric approaches, which claim that the right mental attitude leads to health. These are questions like: What did I do wrong? Do I have spiritual failings? Am I not living joyfully enough? Am I not spiritual enough, authentic enough, loving enough, etc.? Ultimately, these questions are rooted in a feeling of inadequacy, as if being punished for some kind of guilt. These thoughts touch on the concept of "bad karma" —the idea that I must have done something terrible in this life or a past one and now must atone for it through my illness. For some, this may offer a meaningful perspective, where illness and suffering serve a purpose by purifying them for the next life. However, this is not the case for me, and I aim to free myself from these negative, burdensome thought patterns. Yet drawing a clear distinction is not always easy. Throughout this book, seemingly similar thoughts emerge. Yet for me, it's primarily about reflection, examination, and change—not in terms of guilt or wrongdoing as causes of illness, but from the perspective that, if I had to become ill (for whatever reason), I might as well seize the positive opportunities that come with an awareness of mortality.

A ray of hope in this regard came from a passage in *Diary of a Zen Nun* by Nan Shin. In it, she shares similar burdensome thoughts about bad karma related to her cancer. A friend suggested that her illness could be seen as good karma because it deepens her spiritual path. This shift—from seeing illness as guilt and punishment to viewing it as a spiritual impetus—brought about a profound change for Nan Shin. She describes how this perspective allowed her entire being to realign and feel hopeful again, and how profoundly grateful she was to her friend for this insight. For me as well, this perspective has been both helpful and important.

In recent months, as I have grappled with my illness and life journey, I have come to realize that a recurring, fundamental issue keeps arising that often hinders my connection with myself: the feeling that I am not good enough. How can one find peace with oneself while believing they are not good enough? For instance, much of my recurring dissatisfaction in daily life stemmed from placing myself too far behind family concerns, without Julia or anyone else asking it of me. I allowed too little freedom for my own interests, for the things that have long been important to me and still are. It was my own self-imposed standards that caused me to neglect my interests. These self-imposed demands created the feeling that I always needed to be present for my family, that my top priority had to be as a caring and available partner and father. When I didn't receive the same presence in return, I felt disappointed, frustrated, and that it was unfair. I felt as though I was missing out because I placed my needs behind my self-imposed expectations, thereby cutting off parts of my life. Underlying it all was the belief that I wasn't important enough to simply demand what I needed. I had to put myself last, and if anything remained, only then was it acceptable to take it.

A key part of my healing journey has been overcoming this lack of self-worth and learning to accept that I am good enough as I am. The path is challenging, with its ups and downs, but my spiritual practice sustains me. Honestly, I don't truly believe I am "good." I'm well aware of my own failings and flaws. Even Jesus said, "Why do you call me good? No one is good except God alone!" (Mark 10:17-18). Perhaps I don't need to be perfectly good; perhaps it's enough to be good enough just as I am. I find reassurance in the spiritual certainty that I am part of God, and that God loves and accepts me as I am. If I am good enough for God, then surely I should be good enough for myself as well. I reaffirm: I am good enough, and my life belongs solely to me and God.

My spiritual path and healing efforts are, at their core, simple. On the one hand, it involves setting aside daily time and space for personal, contemplative prayer. On the other, it means practicing this conscious connection with God—through calm, love, self-acceptance, gratitude, and mindfulness—in daily life. I feel at the start of what I hope will be a long journey. A life filled with mindful connection, love, gratitude, freedom, insight, and the fulfillment of my unique purpose is, for me, a truly happy and fulfilling one. Regardless of how long it lasts.

Death and Society

Writing a chapter on society is challenging because "society" is an abstract concept encompassing a diverse multitude of individuals. And society is constantly changing. I am part of this society myself, shaped by its influence into the person I am today. I am generally grateful to my society, appreciating its many positive facets. Yet, I find myself questioning certain aspects of this society, as I don't always feel comfortable belonging to it. This discomfort arises from experiences within society and subjective impressions that have shaped my perspective. I'm aware that in this chapter, I am generalizing my subjective image of society and projecting it onto reality. My subjective impressions of society reflect only a small portion of reality and can be applied to society as a whole only in a limited way. Nonetheless, I feel compelled to address the topic of "death and society," sensing that many people in our society are missing something essential. Something essential for people to live happier, more fulfilled lives. I also hope for my society to experience a form of healing, moving toward greater joy, connectedness, and a sense of meaning in life. I hope my reflections may offer some inspiration, even though they are grounded in an imperfect generalization.

My hypothesis may sound unusual, but I believe that what many people lack is an adequate awareness of death. Shortly after my diagnosis, I thought that integrating death and impermanence into daily life would be important and healing—not only for myself but for many in our society. I sense that many people push thoughts of death out of their awareness, avoiding any true confrontation with it. One could almost say that death is collectively suppressed—though that's not entirely accurate, as it has not vanished from societal discourse. Instead, it seems that while death is often considered in abstract terms, it remains absent from our genuine awareness. Death does not evoke anxiety as long as it remains unacknowledged and is not integrated into one's personal reality. Or, as Woody Allen famously remarked, "I'm not afraid of death; I just don't want to be there when it happens." Yet I believe that by excluding death from our lives, we strip life of a fundamental dimension.

Death is an inherent part of life, just as shadow is to light. My journey toward the inevitable end began at birth. Death is natural, yet it terrifies me because I am acutely aware of life's value, constantly threatened by its presence. The thought of becoming "nothing," that my conscious existence could cease, profoundly unsettles me. Death threatens my very being with utter annihilation. For many poets and thinkers, death represents the ultimate source of anxiety. Death is life's unbearable sting. How can we possibly avoid feeling it?

One way to hold death at bay is by pursuing maximum security. In a life that feels completely secure, one need not think about death. We strive to make life as secure as possible, especially in material terms. Ideally, every threat to body and life would be controlled, fostering the impression that even death is, to some extent, within our grasp. For instance, we have largely subdued many of nature's dangers. We have pushed back or eradicated our natural adversaries. Infectious diseases are managed effectively through widely prescribed antibiotics. Vaccines have been developed for a growing number of illnesses, with infants expected to receive most essential vaccinations shortly after birth. There is insurance for nearly every conceivable threat in daily life. We respond to these dangers with an ever-growing array of safety regulations. In the name of security, increased state surveillance and control are continually under consideration. The drive for security permeates modern life.

Through countless technological advancements, we have managed to secure life to an extraordinary degree. In daily life, serious threats to our survival are rare. Today, death has largely become an unusual experience. How many children, teenagers, and even adults in our society have never encountered a deceased person? Thus, death becomes a purely abstract concept, something that no longer truly concerns us.

Yet our sense of security remains constantly under threat. Natural disasters serve as reminders of the limits to our control. We experience crises and wars mostly through the media, yet the fragility of our secure world becomes evident, revealing how powerless logic and reason often are against them. We are constantly concerned about our prosperity, threatened by forces beyond our control. Life's unpredictability, with its unforeseen events, new developments, and emerging threats, remains constant. Life cannot be endlessly controlled by the same methods, as evidenced by the rise of antibiotic-resistant bacteria. The threat to our sense of security may prompt further efforts to strengthen safety, yet it remains inherently fragile. It becomes a cycle of striving for control and safety. This cycle risks placing excessive focus on safety and control, eventually subordinating all else to these priorities. Safety for both body and life, but also financial security—protection of my livelihood. In fact, financial resources are often essential to ensuring security in the first place. The pursuit of security and wealth frequently go hand in hand. When security becomes the highest value, there is a risk that its means—money—will also be prioritized above all else.

We crave security not only in material terms but also in our thoughts and actions. Though our thoughts are free, this freedom can sometimes feel dangerously ungrounded. We seek stability and direction in our thinking, a sense of security about what is right and wrong. We may not always be consciously aware of this need, yet it remains powerful. It can drive us to submit to fanatical ideologies, be they religious or political. I believe a central appeal of fanatical ideologies lies in their promise of security. They offer the correct way to live or the assurance that by following the right faith, one belongs to the chosen community destined for paradise in the afterlife. Some thinkers propose that humanity created religion and the afterlife belief primarily to cope with the fear of death.

Humans have a fundamental psychological need for control, orientation, and security. Without them, even the ordinary challenges of daily life can leave us feeling helpless, leading to heightened stress reactions. A lack of perceived control may contribute to the onset of depression. Often unconsciously, we are willing to pay a high price to maintain our sense of control. In everyday life, we are generally untroubled by the fact that our sense of control is often unrealistic and illusory. We tend to overestimate our influence over the world and its outcomes, mistakenly believing that if we do everything right, nothing bad will happen to us (in psychology, this is called the "It won't happen to me" effect). Though this unrealistic self-assessment is not inherently harmful, it can lead us to blame those who face misfortune, as if they were somehow at fault. For instance, if we hear about a car accident with severe injuries, we might instinctively assume the victim was speeding, inattentive, or perhaps intoxicated. In psychology, this is known as the "blaming the victim" effect. It gives us the comforting belief that bad things won't happen to us, as we would never behave in the same way. In satisfying our psychological need for security, we may unwittingly cast blame on those who actually need our support and compassion. Through the lens of reason, we sacrifice our humanity in exchange for a sense of security.

I have no doubt that security is important. We require a sense of security, and our desire for it has been a primary driver of research and progress, sparking numerous innovations. The pursuit of control and security is, at its core, sensible. The issue, as I see it, is not our need for security, but the extent to which we pursue it. The real question is how aware we are that security can conflict with other values, and whether we recognize that we may be sidelining those values when security becomes too central in our lives.

Our lives are shaped by opposites, where one value frequently stands in contrast to another. Security and freedom, for instance, often come into conflict. In the security provided by fanatical ideologies, there is no space left for freedom of thought or judgment. Similarly, the physical space that provides the highest level of security (like the bunker beneath the White House) is also a place where freedom is severely restricted. It becomes a prison of safety. Conversely, the life of an adventurer in the jungle might symbolize ultimate freedom, but it forsakes nearly all security. In our modern society, increasing safety regulations and state control may enhance security by preventing accidents and making rescues more feasible. Yet this also imposes restrictions on how life can be lived. I often hear those around me say that our society has become so overregulated that there is scarcely any room left for creative freedom.

Freedom is among the central and most potent concepts of human existence. There are situations where people hold their freedom dearer than life itself. Many other values essential to our existence are intrinsically tied to freedom. When security and prosperity dominate our hierarchy of values, they endanger freedom and, with it, other core values of our humanity. It touches upon nothing less than our self-understanding, our human dignity, and values like vitality, spontaneity, creativity, love, meaning, and happiness. The contradictions within our value systems ultimately remain unresolved, and I'd like to illustrate this with two examples from my own life where I personally encounter these conflicts. There are no universal solutions, though I've developed my own clear stance on the matter. It's essential to me to recognize these conflicts, so that we avoid unconsciously making significant sacrifices in favor of security.

During the COVID-19 pandemic, people in our society were abruptly confronted with death, and many experienced profound fear. As a result, there was a rush for swift, maximum security, even when the rationale and likelihood of success were questionable. In my opinion, some measures were taken that went against humanity. How many people were isolated for their own protection, only to suffer loneliness or even die alone against their will? I believe the psychological toll of these protective measures was underestimated. The subsequent rise in suicide rates and the increased demand for psychotherapy speak volumes. Many people were stripped of their livelihoods for choosing not to be vaccinated, with the intent of pressuring them into compliance and thereby enhancing security. However, the relevance of the vaccine's protective effect was as uncertain as its potential long-term negative consequences. How many people were discredited and publicly shamed for adopting a critical stance? I heard people in my own circle say that so-called anti-vaxxers "deserved to rot in hell." To me, it seemed that fear had created second-class citizens, whose right to life was forfeited because of their critical stance. People were categorized by their vaccination status and no longer treated equally, despite the principle that everyone deserves equal treatment. Vaccinated individuals lived with a sense of perceived security, grounded in a supposedly scientific ideology, while vaccine skeptics equally adhered to a view shaped by fear of the vaccine and a desire for security. Both sides resorted to similar forms of devaluation and hostility toward one another. Both sides contributed to deep divisions, threatening to erode solidarity and humanity. Whether the security measures were justified remains an open question to this day.

Supposedly, human health is the highest good, and our healthcare system aims to provide the best possible care for society. In reality, however, our healthcare system often prioritizes security—both financial and legal—above all else. Only funded treatments can be pursued, even if they are not always the best therapies. It ultimately comes down to financial interests and what the insurance system permits. Healthcare institutions must remain financially sustainable, as the financial security of many workers, along with shareholder interests, often depends on them. Healthcare institutions compete for limited financial resources, ultimately pitting health against money. Institutions that seek to survive the competition must be both cost-effective and efficient, while still delivering dividends to shareholders. To accomplish this, they must make cuts somewhere—whether in food, equipment, staff, or a combination of these. How can quality be maintained without it ultimately coming at the expense of patients or employees? Proponents of this system might argue that it works and is effective. Having worked within this system for many years, however, I know from personal experience that many patients and employees in hospitals, rehabilitation centers, and nursing homes feel quite differently. Money takes precedence over everything—even over humanity and dignity, as many doctors and nurses would attest. Today, caregivers often cannot provide the level of care their patients deserve due to tight schedules, and delivering such care would be too costly. If they attempt to do so, they risk burnout or even losing their jobs. Similarly, doctors today often cannot choose the treatment they consider best for their patients. On the one hand, they are bound by standardized guidelines, designed to ensure optimal treatment but often overlooking the complexity of individual cases. If a doctor deviates from these guidelines and the treatment fails—which is always possible—they face serious consequences. On the other hand, the financial stability of the healthcare "business" is always in the background, often giving the hospital manager the final say. Numerous reports question whether every intensive medical intervention truly serves the patient's best interests or primarily aims to secure the institution's financial well-being. In my view, the state failed by relegating the healthcare system to the private market.

Another central drive in our lives is happiness—or, more precisely, the pursuit of a fulfilling life. We seek not only a secure life but also a happy one. Yet I wonder whether a life lacking even minimal security can truly be a happy one. Conversely, I also wonder if a life centered on security necessarily leads to happiness, or if an excess of security might actually hinder it. At its core, there are various paths to happiness. I believe there are paths to happiness that align with security and control, and others that are less compatible. Moreover, I believe that the quality of happiness varies depending on the chosen path. Some paths lead to fleeting moments of superficial happiness, while others lead to a deeper, more fulfilling life, though they may take longer to attain.

One form of happiness lies in "having"—through material possessions and wealth. Fulfilling a heartfelt wish, buying something we desire, something that brings us joy or appeals to our sense of beauty, offers a brief feeling of happiness. Moreover, material possessions and wealth form part of our safety net. However, once we own something, we usually wish to keep and protect it. The more we possess, the greater our fear of losing it. Thus, paradoxically, increased security goes hand in hand with a new sense of fear, which can only be temporarily eased by accumulating even more material security. It becomes a potentially escalating process. What was initially intended as a reassuring safety net, enabling us to focus on other things and enjoy life, becomes the central focus of life itself. Our possessions come to possess us, as Schopenhauer illustrated with his metaphor of salt water: the more you drink, the thirstier you become. Since material goods are limited, greater wealth for one person means less for another. The pursuit of having leads to competition for these limited resources, resulting in injustice and suffering.

Another path to happiness lies in the happiness of "appearance". I may feel happy for a short time when I stand out in the eyes of others and receive special recognition—whether through success, fame, beauty, exceptional achievements, or extraordinary intelligence. The pursuit of appearance leads to comparisons with others in a contest of "I am better than you." It results in a focus on oneself, one's uniqueness, fostering separation rather than connection. My interpretation may be somewhat simplified, yet I sense that "appearance and having" are major sources of suffering in the world—sources of poverty, exploitation, war, chronic stress, and feelings of inadequacy.

I would liken these two paths to building on sand. It may work and support us for a time, but it will not endure. What we gain can be lost—whether possessions, beauty, or fame. This type of happiness remains perpetually threatened by impermanence. There is a third path to happiness that centers on the qualities of being. This path aims more toward a fulfilling life, focusing not on what I have or can lose, but on what I must be as a person.

Viktor Frankl captures this well with the idea that humans are beings who must continually decide who they are. It centers on human qualities like love, compassion, kindness, courage, dignity, respect, authenticity, connectedness, mindfulness, helpfulness, grace, calm, and more. Happiness arises when I am deeply connected to others with love or when I mindfully experience the present moment. Life can be fulfilling despite hardship, sustained by a dignified attitude that defies suffering. These human qualities do not rely on possessions or status. They may be even easier to realize when one has less. And maybe that's why people in other countries who live with far less wealth often seem so much happier than we do, as long as they are not in severe need. I am inclined to agree with Schopenhauer, who was convinced that only the third path leads to true happiness.

What does all of this have to do with me and my experience of illness? Reflecting on the past 15 years of my life, I recognize a growing focus on security. As a young adult, material things held little importance for me. During my university years, until I was 27, I lived on roughly 900 euros per month. What mattered to me was living in a nice shared apartment, spending time with friends, doing activities together, studying psychology and philosophy, and having essentials like a computer with a printer, climbing shoes, and a bicycle. I was covered by my father's family health insurance, but beyond that, I had no other coverage or savings. My safety net was minimal, yet my life was carefree and happy.

After university, I met Julia and began my first job,

which required a car and the necessary insurance. Before long, we added other supplementary insurance policies, like liability and accident insurance. Even so, material security remained secondary; we mostly worked part-time, and saving money was not a priority. We lived mostly carefree, focusing on our relationship, friends, outings, and sports. But when our children were born, things slowly began to shift. Gradually, we added sensible insurance policies—disability insurance, accident insurance for the children, supplementary health insurance, and retirement plans. Today, I spend more each month on this safety net than I had to live on during my university years. With the arrival of children came the need for more space and the desire for the security of owning a home. However, along with the benefits and luxury of homeownership came increased obligations. Working part-time was no longer feasible. To manage daily life with three children and both of our jobs in a rural area, we needed two cars. We wanted the best for our children, and their safety became a priority. We ensured they had wholesome food and high-quality equipment, and so forth. Within a few years, we found ourselves in a cycle that increasingly shifted my focus toward work and financial security—until the day of my diagnosis. My feeling of safety vanished.

At the beginning of this book, I used the metaphor of a path and described my sense of having gone astray at some point. That I was no longer on my personal path in life and was on the verge of missing my life's goal. I realized that, over the years, I had gradually veered onto the path of acquisition and material security. I had walked this path of material security successfully—at least until my diagnosis—though I had unknowingly paid a price. Despite growing prosperity, my life felt duller, emptier, more confined—I didn't feel well within. My illness served as a wake-up call, prompting me to question whether the path I was on was still the right one. I might even say that the looming presence of death freed me from these supposed constraints, revealing that my focus should be on life, not on illusory security. It sharpened my awareness of who I truly am and who I am meant to be.

I believe it is often life's hardships that awaken us and reveal what truly matters. This was true for me, and this theme runs throughout the entire book. This idea is also supported by research on the phenomenon of post-traumatic growth. Be it illness, accidents, natural disasters, wars, or other crises, it ultimately always involves confronting our mortality and the fragility of existence. Such confrontations can heighten our awareness of life's essential questions. Death reminds us that striving for material security, ever-growing wealth, or social status is ultimately meaningless.

Following my terminal diagnosis, material possessions and security became largely irrelevant. For me, security was no longer an option. I was fully aware that I couldn't take anything with me. In my mind's eye, I could already envision all the things I held dear being either passed on or discarded. The house, my cars, my books, my PhD—all of it held little meaning. Death, standing at my door and waiting for me, made it clear that none of it was lasting or significant.

This experience is well illustrated in a quote often attributed to Steve Jobs, the billionaire co-founder of Apple, supposedly spoken shortly before his death from cancer. Officially, the authenticity of the quote is in doubt. In my view, however, it matters little whether these words were truly spoken by Steve Jobs. If there is truth in these words, then that truth exists independently of the speaker. According to the quote, Steve Jobs said:

"I have reached the pinnacle of success in the business world. In the eyes of others, my life is a success. However, aside from work, I have had little joy. Ultimately, wealth is just a fact of life to which I have become accustomed. At this moment, lying on my sickbed and recalling my whole life, I realize that all the recognition and wealth I was so proud of has faded and become meaningless in the face of impending death. You can hire someone to drive your car or make money for you, but it's impossible to hire someone to endure illness and death on your behalf. Lost material things can be recovered, but there is one thing that can never be found once it's lost—life. No matter what stage of life we're in, eventually the curtain will come down. Love your family, your spouse, and your friends. Treat them well and cherish them. As we grow older and wiser, we gradually realize that whether we wear a $300 watch or a $30 watch, both tell the same time. Whether we carry a $300 wallet or a $30 wallet, the amount inside remains the same. Whether we drive a $150,000 car or a $30,000 car, the road and distance are the same, and we reach the same destination. Whether we drink a $1,000 bottle of wine or a $10 bottle, the hangover is the same.

Whether the house we live in is 300 or 3,000 square feet, the loneliness is the same. You will realize that true happiness does not come from material things. Whether you travel first class or economy, if the plane goes down, you go down with it. So... I hope you realize, when you have friends, buddies, and old friends, brothers and sisters, with whom you can talk, laugh, chat, sing, talk about north-south-east-west or heaven and earth... that this is true happiness! And one undeniable fact of life: Do not raise your children to be rich. Educate them to be happy. When they grow up, they will know the value of things, not the price."

The essence of this experience may be summed up as follows: wealth and social status lose their meaning in the face of death. What truly matters in the end is love, connection with family and friends, and finding joy in the present moment. Steve Jobs experienced little joy beyond his work, and though he didn't say it explicitly, his reflection on the priorities he set seems tinged with regret.

Steve Jobs came to this realization with the awareness of his impending death. Paradoxically, death provides a gateway to a fulfilled life—as long as it is not too late to live. Only through death do we come to truly appreciate life and its possibilities. As Yalom (14) expresses it: "The way to appreciate life, the way to feel compassion for others, the way to love most deeply, is through the awareness that these experiences are destined to be lost." The present moment gains its true significance only through its transience. In realizing that the perfect bloom will soon wither, we become acutely aware of the preciousness of each fleeting moment. Without finitude, life risks losing its vibrancy and becoming dull. In mythology, immortal gods are often portrayed as bored.

By confronting my own death and the finitude of existence, I developed a deeper sense of connection and compassion for all. I was shaken by the thought that I might soon be gone and the world would simply continue without me. I realized that everyone around me would eventually face the same experience. Everyone ultimately faces this struggle, unless death arrives suddenly and unexpectedly. Death reminds us that, ultimately, we are all the same. It knows no rank or status; before it, we all stand naked. In the face of death, we are simply brothers and sisters. I came to understand the truth of the Buddhist teaching "Tat Tvam Asi" ("That Thou Art"), which encourages recognizing oneself in others and becoming aware of the deep interconnectedness of all beings. Sogyal Rinpoche (15) writes in The Tibetan Book of Living and Dying: "When we finally come to the certainty that we will die and that all other sentient beings will also die, a burning, almost heartbreaking awareness of the fragility and preciousness of each moment and each being can arise in us, and from this can grow a deep, clear, limitless compassion for all beings."

I imagine what a society guided by such awareness and compassion might look like. I believe it would foster more connection, humility, tolerance, joy, and happiness. Such a society would focus less on economic growth and accumulating wealth and more on reducing suffering—for all people, animals, and plants—ensuring that everyone can live a healthy and dignified life. This compassionate society would work to reduce harmful factors in our lives, such as pollution, unhealthy diets, and stress from work or economic pressures on families. It would prioritize justice and refrain from exploiting either people or nature. It would actively counter the excesses of capitalism. I would feel proud to be part of such a society. However, such a society cannot be imposed from above; it must arise from the hearts of individuals.

During my training as a psychologist, I learned that one of my professional responsibilities is to help people overcome their anxiety and live as free from anxiety as possible. Considering the thoughts I have described, I hold a different view. Naturally, overcoming irrational, overwhelming fears is essential to living a fulfilling life. The question is whether a life free from anxiety truly leads to fulfillment? I believe it is important to sensitize people to existential themes like impermanence and death, bringing the anxiety of death into conscious awareness. What truly matters is integrating death—and anxiety—into one's life. Anyone who seeks to confront themselves and life's essential questions must face death and anxiety, and keep it alive. As long as death remains alive in my mind, I examine each day to see if I am living it rightly. In the words of the great Danish existential philosopher Søren Kierkegaard: "This is an adventure that every human being must go through—to learn to be anxious in order that he may not perish either by never having been in anxiety or by succumbing in anxiety".

A truly happy and fulfilling life must integrate anxiety

rather than suppress it. There exists a mutual dependence between the courage to live and the courage to face death. It demands the courage to accept death as part of one's life in order to live freely. Living freely does not necessarily mean disregarding or entirely giving up security. However, a life of freedom requires awareness of values that hold greater importance than mere survival or comfort. Ultimately, it is faith in these values—and our love for them—that enables us to face death courageously and accept it. This faith, ultimately, is what sets us free.

In this sense, my diagnosis arrived at just the right time. The threat of death, in a way, saved me, as it left me time to reflect on my life and take new paths. Yalom (14) captures this thought perfectly: "Though the physicality of death destroys us, the idea of death can save us."

I hope that the idea of death resonates more deeply in our society's consciousness and that people allow themselves to be touched and transformed by it. Because, in the face of death, what remains is what truly matters in life—the things that bring fulfillment and happiness.

Acknowledgments

I am deeply grateful to many people, and while I cannot name each person individually, I hope they feel included and know the significance of their presence in my life. At this moment, however, I want to offer my heartfelt thanks to those who directly accompany me on this journey.

First and foremost, my deepest gratitude goes to my beloved partner, Julia, for her boundless love and unwavering trust in me. She has always given me the freedom to make my own choices, and I never doubted her steadfast support—no matter where our path might lead. She is the greatest gift of my life.

To my children, I am deeply grateful for their pure vitality, their laughter, and their love. They are a constant reminder of what truly matters in life.

To my mother, I am deeply thankful for her loving care and her unwavering belief in my path. Her vibrant example and positive outlook have guided me through many moments of doubt. I thank my father for his constant care, and my sister Martina for her thoughtful presence and the reassurance that I can always rely on her support.

I am deeply thankful to my mother-in-law for her energetic support and the financial security she provides us.

I am deeply grateful to my dear friend Christian for his steady presence and the profound connection we share as lifelong companions. I extend my heartfelt thanks to Timea, Klaus, Robert, and Luna for their support and for reviewing my manuscript. Their invaluable feedback helped me to articulate my thoughts more clearly and gave me the encouragement needed to complete this book.

My heartfelt thanks go to my naturopath, Dagmar, for her compassionate companionship through countless hours of infusion therapy, her inspiring perspectives, and her positive, humorous outlook. Time spent with her was always uplifting.

My heartfelt gratitude goes to Karl and Fee for their remarkable dedication, which allows so many to benefit from effective fever therapy. I am also thankful to Georg for his expertise and support in lightening our home environment. Finally, I am grateful to Ludwig for his warmth, humanity, and the assurance of his steadfast support.

References

1. Lackner R. *Zähne und Spagyrik: Ganzheitliche Zahnbetrachtung und spagyrische Therapie.* [Teeth and Spagyric Therapy: A Holistic Approach to Dental Health.] Kulmbach: ML Verlag; 2020.

2. Frankl VE. *Der leidende Mensch: Anthropologische Grundlagen der Psychotherapie.* [The Suffering Human: Anthropological Foundations of Psychotherapy.] Bern: Hogrefe; 2018.

3. Lionni L. *Frederick.* [Frederick.] Weinheim, Basel: Beltz & Gelberg; 2009.

4. Hillesum E. *Das denkende Herz der Baracke: Die Tagebücher 1941 - 1943.* [The Thinking Heart of the Barracks: The Diaries 1941 - 1943.] Freiburg, Basel, Wien: Herder; 2022.

5. Yalom ID. *Existenzielle Psychotherapie. [Existential Psychotherapy.]* Köln: EHP; 2010.

6. Schipperges H. *Lebensqualität im Kranksein. [Quality of Life in Illness.]* In: Seifert G, Hrsg. *Lebensqualität in unserer Zeit. Modebegriff oder neues Denken? [Quality of Life in Our Time: Buzzword or New Thinking?]* Göttingen: Vandenhoeck & Ruprecht; 1992. S. 111–22.

7. Levine S. *Sein lassen: Heilung im Leben und im Sterben. [Healing into Life and Death.]* Bielefeld: Kamphausen Media GmbH; 2018.

8. Hartl J. *Eden Culture: Ökologie des Herzens für ein neues Morgen. [Ecology of the Heart for a New Tomorrow.]* Freiburg: Verlag Herder; 2021.

9. Tillich P. *Der Mut zum Sein. [The Courage to Be.]* Hamburg: Furche; 1965.

10. Frank A. *Mit dem Willen des Körpers: Krankheit als existenzielle Erfahrung. [At the Will of the Body. Reflections on Illness.]* Hamburg: Hoffmann und Campe; 1991.

11. Dossey L. *Heilende Worte: Die Kraft der Gebete als Schlüssel zur Heilung. [Healing Words: The Power of Prayer and the Practice of Medicine.]* Amerang: Crotona; 2013.

12. Schüssler W, Reimer AJ, Chun YH. *Das Gebet als Grundakt des Glaubens: Philosophisch-theologische Überlegungen zum Gebetsverständnis Paul Tillichs. [Prayer as a Fundamental Act of Faith: Philosophical-Theological Reflections on Paul Tillich's Understanding of Prayer.]* Münster: Lit; 2004. (Tillich-Studien. BeihefteBd. 2).

13. Shin N. *Diary of a Zen nun.* 1st ed. New York: E. P. Dutton; Dutton; 1986.

14. Yalom ID. *In die Sonne schauen: Wie man die Angst vor dem Tod überwindet. [Staring at the Sun: Overcoming the Terror of Death.]* München: btb; 2010.

15. Rinpoche S. *Das tibetische Buch vom Leben und vom Sterben: Ein Schlüssel zum tieferen Verständnis von Leben und Tod. [The Tibetan Book of Living and Dying: A Spiritual Classic from One of the Foremost Interpreters of Tibetan Buddhism to the West.]* München: Knaur; 2010.

16. Kierkegaard S. *Der Begriff Angst. [The Concept of Anxiety.]* Hamburg: EVA; 2002.